DEVALUATION, THE TRADE BALANCE, AND THE BALANCE OF PAYMENTS

BUSINESS ECONOMICS AND FINANCE

a series of monographs and textbooks

Executive Editor

Arthur B. Laffer

Department of Finance and Business Economics
School of Business Administration
University of Southern California
University Park
Los Angeles, California

1. Common Globe or Global Commons: Population Regulation and Income Distribution, *John C. G. Boot*
2. Lags in the Effects of Monetary Policy: A Nonparametric Analysis, *Gene C. Uselton*
3. Demand for Money in Israel, *Lewis Mandell*
4. Key Issues in International Monetary Reform, *edited by Randall Hinshaw*
5. Private Short-Term Capital Flows, *Arthur B. Laffer*
6. International Trade and Distortions in Factor Markets, *Stephen P. Magee*
7. The Demand for Money by Firms, *C. Robert Coates*
8. Money and Finance in Economic Growth and Development, *edited by Ronald I. McKinnon*
9. Purchasing Power Parity, *Moon H. Lee*
10. Stagflation: An International Problem, *edited by Randall Hinshaw*
11. Devaluation, the Trade Balance, and the Balance of Payments, *Marc A. Miles*

Other Volumes in Preparation

DEVALUATION, THE TRADE BALANCE, AND THE BALANCE OF PAYMENTS

Marc A. Miles
Department of Economics
Rutgers College
Rutgers University
New Brunswick, New Jersey

MARCEL DEKKER, INC. New York and Basel

Library of Congress Cataloging in Publication Data

Miles, Marc A., [Date]
Devaluation, the trade balance, and the balance of payments.

(Business economics and finance ; v. 11)
Bibliography: p.
Includes index.
1. Foreign exchange problem. 2. Currency question. 3. Balance of trade. 4. Balance of payments. I. Title.
HG3826.M48 332.4'5 78-7550
ISBN 0-8247-6666-0

MARCEL DEKKER, INC.
270 Madison Avenue, New York, New York 10016

Current printing (last digit):
10 9 8 7 6 5 4 3 2

PRINTED IN THE UNITED STATES OF AMERICA

FOR MANJA

PREFACE

The current regime of frequently fluctuating exchange rates serves as a focus for renewed discussions over the precise effects of currency depreciation. On one side of the issue are those who feel that currency depreciation provides positive employment effects and eventually improves the trade balance. On the other side are those who feel that currency depreciation has little if any effect on the net production or consumption of goods, but rather causes primarily only portfolio readjustments and increased inflation. Both sides have theoretical arguments to justify their positions. The issue obviously needs to be resolved on empirical grounds.

Since exchange rates were fixed during most of the period over which the necessary data exist, the empirical study of currency depreciation has concentrated on the effects of once-for-all devaluations. However, as one investigates the empirical work on devaluation, one is struck by the lack of an in-depth study of the effects of devaluation on the foreign balances. Studies employing sophisticated statistical techniques concentrate on the effects of devaluation on only exports, imports, market shares, or similar measures, not on the trade balance itself. Those schooled in general equilibrium theory can appreciate that the behavior of one component may not describe the behavior of the entire account. Furthermore, studies which do evaluate the behavior of the trade balance and/or balance of payments following devaluation fail to separate the effects of devaluation from the effects of other policy tools or economic variables which are also changing at the time. All changes in the accounts are simply ascribed to devaluation. In short, the empirical issue of the effects of devaluation on the foreign balances has barely been scratched.

The purpose of this book is to aid the resolution of this empirical issue. The primary goal is fairly simple: determine the effect of devaluation on the trade balance and balance of payments over as many devaluations as possible, after first standardizing for the effects of other economic policies. Attainment of the goal has required a few restrictions. For example, I was unable to delve into the specific conditions existing within the countries during each of the twenty-six devaluations included in the study. However, the size of the sample does permit me to infer that the results indicate what on average happens to the foreign balances following devaluation. I believe the reader will find the results both revealing and provocative.

I would like to thank especially Arthur Laffer for helpful and incisive comments and discussions throughout the development of this book. He has made available to me a disproportionate amount of his time, not only during the writing of this book, but during all the years of our acquaintance. I am greatly indebted to him for his continued confidence and support. Thanks are also extended to Jacob Frenkel, Stephen Magee, John Bilson, Rudiger Dornbush and the late Harry Johnson for their comments and ideas. Any errors, however, must remain my burden.

Carol Harvey assisted me in the preparation of the index. Betty Hafner and Gerri Dructor typed the manuscript at different stages of production. Each performed proficiently in their assignments, and I thank them for their diligence.

On a more personal note, I would like to thank my wife Manja for the emotional and financial support she has provided me throughout my graduate and professional years. Her insight and frequent advice have helped me to keep sight of my goals even during the toughest periods. Appreciation is also extended to our cat Bayswater who somehow always knew when to provide levity and diversionary relief from long hours of writing.

Marc A. Miles

CONTENTS

LIST OF ILLUSTRATIONS

LIST OF TABLES

Chapter I

INTRODUCTION

The exchange rate has traditionally been considered an important governmental policy instrument. Changes in exchange rates, particularly devaluations, have therefore become the subject of lengthy discussions within the academic, business and government communities. The description of the expected quantitative effects of devaluation in these discussions can be divided into two basic categories. The first concentrates primarily on the income and employment effects of an improved trade balance, while the second concentrates principally on the effect of an increase in the level of international reserves through an improved balance of payments. Historically, the income and employment effects of increased net exports have dominated the analysis. It was not until the last decade with the rediscovery of the Monetary Approach to the Balance of Payments that the second category emerged as a separate, independent method of analyzing the impact of devaluation.

The traditional or popularly held view of the impact of devaluation is therefore centered around potential income and employment effects. This rationale for the use of devaluation as a policy instrument is by now familiar to anyone who reads the newspaper. Devaluation is viewed as a method of improving a country's "competitiveness", or in other words rendering domestically produced goods more attractive abroad while making foreign produced goods less attractive at home. This shift in the attractiveness of traded goods causes the level of exports to rise, the level of imports to fall, the trade balance to improve and domestic employment to increase. Indeed, this was precisely the justification for the round of "beggar-thy-neighbor" devaluations of the 1930's. Many countries, facing massive domestic unemployment, decided to devalue their currencies in the hope of alleviating these domestic pressures. Not surprisingly, theoretical writings of the 30's reflect this pro-employment belief concerning the effects of devaluation. Writing about possible remedies for the unemployment problem, Joan Robinson states[1]:

> A fall in the exchange rate, or in money wages, causes a primary increase in employment in export industries, and in industries producing goods rival to imports. For a given increase in the value of exports (in terms of home wage units) the increase in employment will be greater the greater is the elasticity of supply, and for a given decrease in the value of imports it will be greater the greater is the elasticity of foreign supply and the greater is the elasticity of supply in the rival home industries.

These same arguments, transmitted into contemporary thought, are still influencing economic policy decision-making. In defending the devaluation of the dollar in 1971 President Nixon stated that[2]:

---

1 Joan Robinson, "Beggar-My-Neighbour Remedies for Unemployment," reprinted in H. Ellis and L. Metzler ed., Readings in the Theory of International Trade, Philadelphia: Blakiston, 1949, P. 397.

2 Richard M. Nixon, "The Challenge of Peace," a radio and television address of August 15, 1971, in Weekly Compilation of Presidential Documents for week ending August 21, 1971.

> .... As a result of these actions, the product of American labor will be more competitive, and the unfair edge that some of our foreign competition has will be removed. This is a major reason why our trade balance has eroded over the past 15 years[3] .... But now that other nations are economically strong, the time has come for them to bear their fair share of the burden of defending freedom around the world. The time has come for exchange rates to be set straight and for the major nations to compete as equals. There is no longer any need for the United States to compete with one hand tied behind her back.

On the other hand, the Monetary Approach concentrates less on the employment effects of devaluation and more on its basic monetary nature. Through its impact on the value of portfolio holdings of money and bonds, devaluation is thought to generate redistribution of assets among countries which in turn leads to an inflow of international reserves. While primary emphasis is placed on the movement of financial assets, the theory can also be utilized to illustrate a variety of possible effects on the trade balance.

Given the sizable amount of effort expended in attempts to explain the effects of devaluation on the trade balance or balance of payments, it is surprising how little time has actually been devoted to empirically analyzing the results of previous devaluations. While some studies indicate whether the trade balance improves or worsens, little if any effort has been made to determine the duration of any improvement (deterioration) or even whether the change can be ascribed solely to devaluation. As a consequence of this dearth of empirical studies, knowledge of

---

[3] The President was also referring here to reasons for imposing a ten percent surtax on import duties. The traditional argument for tariffs, however, is the same as that for devaluation, i.e., improve the trade balance by making foreign goods more expensive. The fact that both devaluation and a tariff were used as policies therefore only reinforces the point being made.

what to expect on average following devaluation is extremely scanty and incomplete.

This book attempts to eliminate that gap in our knowledge. Starting from a general-equilibrium, theoretical model that includes both goods and financial assets, the possible effects of devaluation under various theoretical assumptions are outlined. These theoretical implications in turn provide hypotheses which are tested in the second part of the book over a sample of twenty-six devaluations. These empirical tests, however, are not performed in a vacuum. The tests are constructed to first remove in each individual country the effects of government policies as well as the impact from other variables which could simultaneously affect the foreign accounts being analyzed. By standardizing for the other exogenous variables in this manner, the effect of devaluation can be isolated to an extent that has not been previously achieved.

The results of the empirical tests are quite informative and interesting. There is little evidence to support the widely held belief that devaluation improves the trade balance. While there appears to be a slight improvement on average in the year following devaluation, this improvement is smaller than the average deterioration that occurs in the year of devaluation. There is no evidence in the year following devaluation of net improvement in the trade balance over the pre-devaluation levels, nor does a net improvement appear within the next two years. In contrast, based on these tests the hypothesis that devaluation causes the balance of payments to improve cannot be rejected. The balance of payments is shown to improve sufficiently in the year following devaluation to become more positive or less negative than in the preceding years. However, there is also some evidence that the improvement is only temporary, lasting about two years and providing a "stock" adjustment of portfolios.

These results contain at least two important implications concerning the effects of devaluation. First, the failure to find evidence that the trade balance improves raises serious questions about the relevance of either competitiveness or wealth transferring arguments for devaluation. Second, since the trade balance does not improve but the balance of payments does, by definition the capital account must be improving. The primary effect of devaluation appears to be on financial assets, causing an inflow of money and an outflow of bonds. Devaluation therefore appears to cause no more than an adjustment of financial portfolios. These results are also consistent with the hypothesis to be discussed later in the book that fiat money does not represent net wealth.

Chapter II of the book presents the theoretical model and outlines some of the theoretical questions to be investigated. Issues such as whether fiat money is net wealth are discussed and the implications of such assumptions are noted. Chapter III summarizes previous empirical studies of the effects of devaluation on the trade balance and balance of payments. Emphasis is placed on the results of these studies and how their methodology differs from the methodology employed here.

The empirical results are contained in Chapters IV - VIII. In Chapter IV the basic functional forms used in the tests are explained and described. The functional forms are then tested on a group of countries not in the devaluation sample. The same functional forms are then applied to the devaluing countries. Chapter V describes the results from testing the effect of devaluation on the trade balance, while the effect on the balance of payments is shown in Chapter VI. In order to examine the sensitivity of these initial results, additional tests are performed on both the trade balance and balance of payments in Chapter VII. Finally, Chapter VIII summarizes the results of all the tests and discusses the implications.

Chapter II

THEORETICAL MODELS OF DEVALUATION

INTRODUCTION

This chapter examines some theories of devaluation to determine what assumptions are necessary in order for real effects to occur. Real effects require a change in a real variable. The exchange rate, however, is a nominal variable. It represents the relative value of two countries' currencies. A country's currency is the numeraire in which the country's goods are denominated. Changing the exchange rate is therefore equivalent to a relative change in units of two numeraires. Such an accounting change should ideally produce only nominal effects. If the relative value of a country's numeraire is reduced by x%, all prices should simply rise by x% in terms of the new numeraire. As long as all demand and supply functions are homogeneous of degree zero in nominal prices and expenditure, and all nominal prices and assets are free to adjust to the new numeraire, no real effects should appear. In a "stroke of a pen" the country can return to its previous equilibrium.

Yet many theories of devaluation predict that real effects will follow a change in the exchange rate. These real effects must be caused by other real variables changing. The source of these real changes must be determined. In the next section of this chapter a general-equilibrium model where no real effects occur is described. The assumptions of this model are carefully examined to determine why no real changes occur. In the following three sections alternative models are presented. Each of these models changes an assumption about the adjustment of an asset or prices, or how individuals discount their future liabilities. Changing these assumptions changes the initial model sufficiently to produce a prediction of real effects following devaluation. The exact cause of the change in prediction is fully analyzed. The next section of the chapter describes the effects of introducing the possibility of nominally-denominated capital assets within these models. Finally, the last section summarizes the models and their implications for the foreign accounts. How well the predictions correspond to actual experience is tested in subsequent chapters.

A FRAMEWORK FOR ANALYZING THE EFFECTS OF DEVALUATION

In order for a real effect such as a change in the trade balance to occur, another real variable in the system must change. Without such an initial real change, only nominal adjustments can occur. For example, suppose the domestic real demand function for any traded good x_i is

$$x_i = f(P_i, P_j, E) \tag{2.1}$$

where P_i and P_j are the prices of x_i and all other goods x_j, and E is the domestic nominal level of expenditure. If the function is homogeneous of degree zero in nominal prices and expenditure, then increasing all nominal variables proportionally yields

$$\lambda^0 x_i = g(\lambda P_i, \lambda P_j, \lambda E). \tag{2.2}$$

In other words, there are no real effects. The real demand for x_i is unchanged.

The only way that real effects can occur is for at least one of the arguments in the real demand function (2.1) not to change in proportion to the remaining two. Such a non-proportional adjustment can occur in three ways. The first is through a change in relative prices, i.e., a change in the terms of trade. A relative price change may sufficiently affect the demand and supply of goods to at least temporarily produce a real change. The two remaining effects occur directly through the level of expenditure. The domestic level of nominal expenditure can be described by

$$E = P \cdot h(w,d) \qquad (2.3)$$

where P is the domestic price level, w is the domestic level of real wealth and d is a vector of marginal propensities to expend of the inhabitants of the country. The two remaining effects are therefore caused by changes in w or differing values within d. For example, suppose that a rise in prices by x% causes real wealth to fall. While the price level in (2.3) rises by x%, the nominal level of expenditure will not. The fall in real wealth w causes real expenditure to fall. Nominal expenditure increases less than proportionately to other variables. Differing values of d create the possibility of distribution effects. If the elements of d differ and the price rise causes redistribution of wealth, say from debtors to creditors, then the real demand for goods may change and real effects will be observed.

In this section of the chapter, a framework is developed in which none of these real effects occur. In order to eliminate the real effects, a specific set of assumptions must be made. These assumptions eliminate real effects due to d, the P's and w. The first assumption is that all individuals are assumed to react in the same way at the margin. This restriction is equivalent to assuming that all elements of d in (2.3) are identical. A second assumption is that the prices of all goods adjust according to

$$\dot{P} = \dot{e} + \dot{P}^* \tag{2.4}$$

where P and P* are the domestic and foreign prices respectively, e is the exchange rate and a "•" indicates a percentage change. The first assumption eliminates the possibility of domestic distribution effects. Redistributing wealth no longer can change overall demand. The second assumption eliminates the possibility of domestic relative price changes. If the first assumption is further extended by assuming all individuals in all countries behave the same at the margin, the possibility of even terms of trade effects can be eliminated. Terms of trade effects occur because relative world demand for goods changes. A possible cause of changes in relative demand following devaluation is a transfer of wealth between two countries with different aggregate marginal propensities to expend (see Mundell, 1968, Dornbusch, 1973a). Assuming all individuals to have the same marginal propensities eliminates this possibility.

Once the assumptions about prices and marginal propensities have been made, the only remaining source of real effects is through changes in real wealth. The effect of real wealth on the trade balance can be seen through the absorption equation

$$TB = P \cdot Y - E(P,w), \tag{2.5}$$

where TB is the nominal trade balance, Y is the real level of domestic production, E is the nominal level of domestic expenditure, P is the domestic price level and w is the level of real wealth. Since real expenditure is assumed to be a positive function of real wealth, given the price level the greater real wealth, the greater the level of nominal expenditure. By determining what is wealth and how it is changing, the path of the trade balance can be determined.

If there has been no international trade in capital, the trade balance surplus (deficit) represents the net increase (decrease) in the country's wealth position. All resources are domestically owned in this case, and the level of domestic production represents the budget constraint for a country. If all goods domestically produced are domestically consumed, there are no goods remaining to be traded for foreign (money) assets. If, however, not all domestically produced goods are consumed, the country is expending at a rate less than its budget constraint and the remaining goods can be traded for foreign assets. The domestic level of wealth increases, the domestic level of expenditure increases, and the rate of wealth accumulation falls.

Where international capital transactions exist, the relationship is slightly more complicated. The trade balance still represents the difference between domestic production (GDP) and the domestic level of expenditure. But since GDP no longer represents the country's budget constraint, the trade balance no longer represents the rate of wealth accumulation. The country's budget constraint now consists of two components, domestic production and net income from abroad. The net income from abroad is the net return from foreign capital investments. The country's budget constraint is now represented by its GNP. Countries which are net creditors on international capital markets will receive income from abroad and have budget constraints which exceed domestic production. Countries which are net debtors will have expendable incomes less than their domestic production. The change in a country's wealth can be represented by the current account

$$CA = P \cdot Y - E(P,w) \quad (2.6)$$

where CA is the nominal current account and Y now represents GNP. Domestic expenditure will rise with current account surpluses and fall with deficits.

While the path of the foreign accounts which will be examined in the analysis represent private actions, these private actions depend not just upon private wealth, but upon the consolidated wealth position of the country, i.e., including the government. One portion of the government's wealth is its stock of foreign reserves. As shown by Black (1973), these reserves are typically not held in the form of foreign currency balances. Rather central banks hold their reserves in the form of interest-bearing, foreign currency-denominated bonds. When additional liquid reserves are needed, these bonds are simply sold abroad and the proceeds are used to settle the foreign currency obligations.

The fact that reserves are held as foreign currency, interest-bearing bonds has two important implications for the present analysis. The first is that it helps explain why the consolidated balance sheet is important in determining a country's behavior. The fact that the government owns interest-bearing foreign bonds may at first appear to have no effect on domestic private wealth or behavior. But increased bond holdings imply increased interest income for the government. With constant government expenditures, the government can now meet its outlays with smaller domestic tax revenues. In other words, the bond holdings by the government have increased private wealth through reduced tax liabilities. Furthermore, if we assume markets are efficient, the discounted value of reduced tax liabilities will just equal the discounted value of the interest payments, i.e., the value of the bonds themselves. So not only does private wealth rise when the government holds bonds, but private wealth rises by exactly the value of the bonds.

The second implication of holding bonds as reserves is in the way surpluses on the various accounts are viewed. For example, a combined capital account and balance of payments surplus does not represent a net inflow of foreign currency and a net outflow of bonds. Rather the net effect is to increase only the supply of domestic currency. To illustrate this point, suppose France has such a surplus with the United States. Frenchmen have exchanged some of their bond holdings for dollars. However, Frenchmen are assumed to execute their domestic transactions only in francs, not dollars. Thus they must turn these dollars into the French central bank for francs. If the French central bank were happy to hold non-interest-bearing dollars, we would at this point have the traditional result that a capital account-balance of payments surplus is associated with a net inflow of foreign reserves, and a net outflow of bonds. But since the central bank will want to hold interest-bearing bonds instead, the net result is different. The central bank's dollars are now exchanged abroad for bonds. There has been an inflow and outflow of dollars, an inflow and outflow of bonds and a printing of francs. The two sets of inflows and outflows cancel. The only remaining effect is the printing of francs. It will be shown below that a capital account-balance of payments surplus therefore implies no change in net wealth.

A current account surplus can be associated with a balance of payments surplus and/or a capital account deficit. If the current account surplus is just matched by the capital account deficit, goods are being exchanged directly for foreign bonds. There is no reason for the governments to intervene since there is no net exchange of money across countries. The current account surplus will simply be accompanied by an equivalent inflow of bonds. However, if the current account surplus is just matched by a balance of payments surplus, the central bank will have to intervene. In this case the goods are being exchanged only for foreign money, and the central bank will intervene to exchange domestic for foreign currency. The foreign currency will then be used to purchase foreign-denominated bonds. The inflow of bonds is accompanied by printing money. An intermediate case is a combination of the two cases above. In any of these cases the current account surplus will cause an increase in net domestic wealth and a rise in domestic expenditure as individuals discount the value of their reduced tax liabilities. Thus a current account surplus continues to represent an excess of savings over investment, or a net accumulation of wealth.

The discounting of future values is assumed to be symmetric in this model. Not only reduced future tax liabilities but also increased future tax liabilities are assumed to be perfectly foreseen and discounted at the market rate of interest. The discounting of future tax liabilities becomes particularly important when the government is constrained to follow an optimal monetary policy. The combination of the policy constraint and the discounting of liabilities results in domestic currency no longer being considered net wealth.

Recall that the foreign currency-denominated bonds that accompany a current account surplus are considered net wealth. The foreign bonds represent a domestic asset in the form of a discounted stream of interest payments. There is no offsetting domestic liability because the sources of interest payments are all abroad. Domestic currency also represents an asset. The currency represents a store of value that can be exercised at some later period. But the currency also has an offsetting domestic liability associated with it. To see where this liability comes from it is first necessary to discuss the behavior of the central bank over time.

Most models of monetary policy, both closed (e.g., Patinkin, 1965, Friedman, 1969) and open economy models (e.g., Mundell, 1968, Dornbusch, 1973a, Johnson, 1972), assume that monetary policies among different time periods are essentially independent. A two percent increase in the money supply this period has no effect on the decision to have a six percent increase in some later period. Each period's monetary policy is assumed to be exogenous and to depend only upon the whims of the central bank at the moment. But such an assumption ignores completely the fact that there may be an optimal monetary policy which the central bank should be pursuing. Under this assumption increased supplies of money are assumed to increase domestic net wealth. The argument is that these printed pieces of paper represent assets, but since they never will be retired, there are no offsetting liabilities.

As long as monetary policies are assumed to be independent among periods, the wealth assumption may be reasonable. There must exist, however, an optimal monetary policy. One candidate for an optimal policy is one which keeps all prices including the interest rate constant. Thus all countries should be running budget deficits at a rate which allows them to maintain a constant per capita ratio of money to bonds. In other words the optimal monetary and bond policies will be tied to the domestic growth rates.

Once the optimal monetary policy is recognized, however, monetary policy in different periods of time are no longer independent, and an explicit liability becomes associated with each asset. Over a given period of time, the number of created units of currency consistent with optimal policy is constrained by the rate of growth. Thus for every unit of currency issued this period, one fewer unit can be issued in some future period. The same argument holds for the issuing of bonds as a means of deficit financing. So for every unit of currency and bonds issued this period and not retired in a later period, an alternative source of financing must be found for government expenditures in later periods. The alternative source is tax revenues. Thus for every unit of currency or bonds printed now, future tax liabilities rise. In addition to representing a store of value, money also represents a store of tax liabilities. Each asset is associated with an offsetting liability. Even though the assets are never retired, there is no longer any net aggregate wealth value to either type of asset.

The fact that issuing domestic bonds or currency has no net wealth effect has important implications about the impact of foreign account surpluses or deficits on the country's stock of wealth. When countries hold bonds as reserves, the net effect of a capital account-balance of payments surplus is for the country to issue domestic currency. Thus such a surplus or deficit should have no wealth effect. Similarly, a current account surplus will increase wealth only to the extent that it involves the inflow of foreign bonds. This is an important result because it assumes that, as we would expect, the wealth effect will be the same regardless of whether the goods are exchanged for money or bonds. If printing money created wealth, then the form of payment for the good would be important. For example, take equally sized current account surpluses, one accompanied by an equal size capital account surplus (financed entirely by bonds), the other by an equal size balance of payments surplus (financed by foreign currency). From the above analysis, both involve the same increase in holdings of foreign bonds on the country's consolidated balance sheet. Where the goods are exchanged directly for bonds private holdings rise. Where goods are exchanged for foreign currency, government holdings increase. The only difference is that where the goods are exchanged for currency, private holdings of domestic currency also rise. If the domestic currency represented net wealth, then the country's level of wealth would rise more when goods are exchanged for foreign currency than when exchanged directly for bonds. Such asymmetry is undesirable.

A framework has thus been created in which the only domestic source of real wealth can be real assets. The important implication of this framework for devaluation is that devaluation has no net effect on the current account or on the trade balance. Equations (2.5) and (2.6) show that there will be a change in the current account or trade balance only if real expenditure is affected. But the level of real expenditure is assumed to depend on the real wealth level of the consolidated balance sheet, and that has not changed. Since domestic money and bonds represent equal quantities of assets and liabilities denominated in domestic currency, these assets and liabilities will decrease in real value by the same amount. The level of real wealth associated with a given level of domestic nominal assets is unchanged. Under the small country assumption, the real value of foreign bonds should not change either. The real value of capital assets does not change. There is no source of changes in real wealth, and thus no changes in the level of savings relative to investment. The current account and trade balance are unchanged.

The only effect of devaluation in this model is to change the proportion of money to bonds in the country. For example, money represents money assets and tax liabilities (negative bonds). Devaluation reduces the real value of both. Thus money assets decline while bond holdings increase (become less negative). With the interest rate unchanged the actual ratio of money to bonds will be less than the desired ratio.

In order to return the money-bonds ratio to the desired level, the country will run capital account and balance of payments surpluses. As shown above, the net effect of such a surplus is an increase in the domestic money supply. The country's portfolio composition will be returned to the desired level. Net wealth remains unaffected, as does expenditure and the current and trade accounts.

Thus where future tax liabilities are properly discounted devaluation is neutral. There are no real effects. The current account and level of wealth remain unchanged. Following the readjustment of portfolios to the desired money-bond ratio, the only lingering effect will be a rise in the relative domestic price level by the percentage of devaluation. As shown below, any other assumed effect of devaluation requires violation of one of the important assumptions of this model.

RELATING THE FRAMEWORK TO OTHER MODELS

The two conditions that are often assumed away in models of devaluation (e.g., Dornbusch, 1973a, Frenkel and Rodriguez, 1975) are the constraints on the country's monetary and bond policies and the effect of government wealth holdings on private expenditure. Monetary and bond policy decisions in one period are assumed unconstrained by the decisions in any other period. The central bank is assumed free to follow whatever policy currently deemed prudent. Since money and bond production this period does not affect production in any other period, the liabilities associated with issuing either asset disappear. Domestic money and bonds become net wealth.

Similarly, the government's wealth holdings are ignored. Private expenditure is described as depending exclusively on private wealth holdings. These models are therefore assuming that the level of the government's wealth does not affect private wealth. Either the government is continually destroying any wealth it accumulates, or private individuals do not see the government's income as reducing the tax liabilities of the private sector.

The myopic behavior of the private sector leads these models to be solely concerned with private portfolios. The introduction of a nominally-denominated form of net wealth held by the private sector provides a possible source for a change in the real value of such a portfolio, causing an adjustment in the rate of expenditure relative to income, improving the current account and trade balance and causing a net accumulation of assets. Thus the change in only one or two assumptions reintroduces a real effect of devaluation. In order to analyze the implications of a current account improvement under the changed assumptions, a framework is used which simultaneously incorporates changes in excess demand in all private markets. The framework is the portfolio equilibrium model.

The basis of the portfolio equilibrium model is that, given the level of wealth, individuals immediately adjust their assets to the desired ratio of money to other assets. The desired ratio is in turn determined by the prevailing interest rate. The higher the interest rate, the larger the opportunity cost of holding money, and the smaller the desired ratio of money to other assets.

The portfolio model is summarized in Figure 1. The total value of real assets in the economy is a_0, which can be divided between real money and bond holdings in any combination along wealth constraint $a_0 a_o$. The desired level, however, is determined by the liquidity ratio function ℓ and the prevailing interest rate r. Given the level of wealth a_0 and the interest rate r, the desired real asset holdings are b_0 of bonds and m_0 of money.

The portfolio model shows the effect of a current account surplus or deficit on the balance of payments and the capital account. A current account surplus represents the net accumulation of assets. Thus a surplus implies

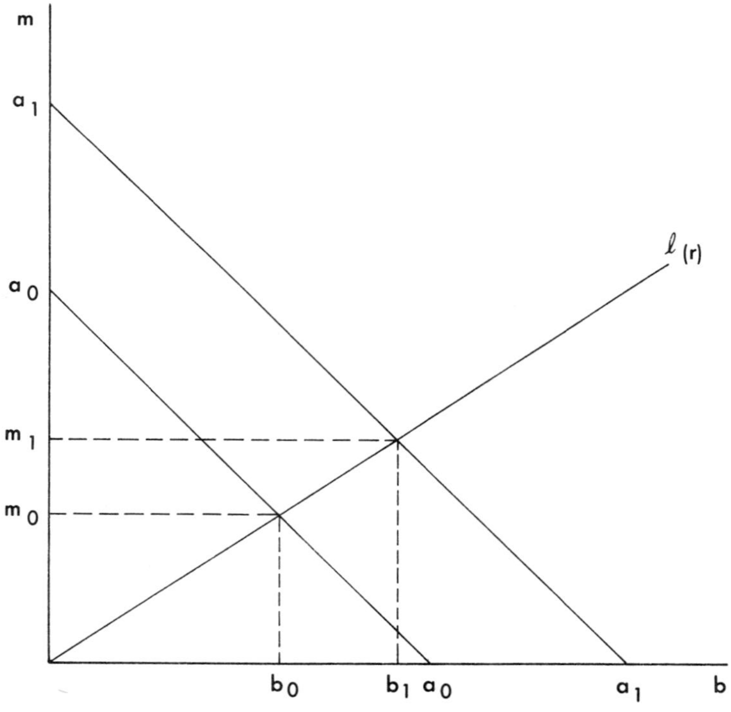

Figure 1: The portfolio equilibrium model.

that the wealth constraint aa will be moving outward in a northeast direction. With the interest rate remaining at r, there is no reason (assuming wealth elasticities equal to one) for the desired asset ratio to change. Thus the equilibrium holdings of assets moves along the ray $\ell(r)$.

For example, suppose a current account surplus shifts the wealth constraint from a_0a_0 to a_1a_1 in Figure 1. Equilibrium asset holdings increase along $\ell(r)$ to m_1 and b_1. The increase in wealth $a_1 - a_0$ measures the level of the current account surplus. The ray $\ell(r)$ measures the ratio of the balance of payments surplus to capital account deficit.

Notice that the portfolio model is inconsistent with the model where all future tax liabilities are foreseen and discounted. In such a model domestically issued money and bonds would not be net wealth. The lines a_0a_0 and a_1a_1 could therefore not describe net wealth. All money balances are in domestic currency, so there will be an offsetting liability for each unit of m. Similarly, for each unit of b that represents domestically issued bonds, there is also an offsetting liability. These liabilities would have to be subtracted from the value of remaining bonds and equities b in order to obtain the net wealth value of capital assets. Thus there is no longer a unique aa line associated with a given level of wealth. If domestic currency is issued, both money assets and bond liabilities increase. Real wealth is unchanged. But the wealth constraint aa initially associated with given real level w has rotated clockwise as m increases and b decreases. In addition the model assumes that portfolio behavior depends exclusively on private sector holdings. No provision is made for the public to discount the future income from the government's stock of foreign bonds. Including the discounting assumptions would therefore render the portfolio graph meaningless.

CONSTANT NOMINAL MONEY SUPPLY

Recall from equation (2.2) that the only way the real changes in the demand for goods can occur is for one of the prices or nominal expenditure not to increase proportionately to the others. Within a model where money is considered to be net wealth, one way the real effects can be achieved is by assuming that the government holds the nominal money supply constant following devaluation. The implications of such an assumption have been described by Frenkel and Rodriguez (1975) and Dornbusch (1973a) within the context of the portfolio model. In the Frenkel-Rodriguez model, two tradable assets are held. One is money, whose value is fixed in nominal terms. The other is shares of equity which represent ownership of machinery or other real investment goods. Devaluation therefore can affect only the real value of the nominal asset money.

Dornbusch uses essentially the same model, except that he adds the existence of a nontradable capital asset. The nontradable asset is assumed to be an imperfect substitute for the traded equity in both demand and supply. The rates of return on the two assets will therefore differ, and it is assumed that the return on the nontradable asset determines the domestic level of savings and investment. Notice that it is the imperfect substitute assumption, not the existence of nontraded assets, which causes the two models to differ. A model containing nontraded assets that are perfect substitutes for the traded equity in either demand or supply would behave exactly the same as the Frenkel-Rodqiguez model as long as the domestic level of demand for capital assets at the world interest rate were at least equal to the existing supply of the nontradable assets.

In these models all consumption goods are assumed to be tradable. The real demand function for any good i can again be described by

$$X_i = g(P_i, P_j, E) \tag{2.1}$$

where the P's are the prices of goods i and j, and E is the nominal level of expenditure. The real supply function is

$$S_i = h(P_i, P_j). \tag{2.7}$$

The demand and supply functions are assumed homogeneous of degree zero in all variables. Thus

$$\lambda^o X_i = g(\lambda P_i, \lambda P_j, \lambda E) \text{ and} \tag{2.2}$$

$$\lambda^0 S_i = h(\lambda P_i, \lambda P_j).$$

Using the small country assumption ($P = eP^*$), devaluation causes all domestic prices to rise by the percentage of devaluation. The real domestic supply of goods therefore remains constant. Real domestic demand also remains constant if nominal expenditure rises by the percentage of devaluation. From equation (2.3), nominal expenditure is a function of real wealth and the price level, or in other words nominal wealth. So as long as nominal wealth does not rise in proportion to the price level, real demand will fall.

Since money holdings are considered part of net wealth, the failure of the government to increase the nominal quantity of money in proportion to the exchange rate change means that nominal holdings of money, and therefore wealth, do not rise proportionately. The relative fall in nominal wealth reduces nominal expenditure relative to income and creates a current account surplus. The relative reduction in money holdings may also cause the actual money to bonds ratio to deviate from the desired ratio, thus requiring a portfolio readjustment as well.

The adjustment process is described by Frenkel and Rodriguez in terms of the portfolio diagram (Figure 2). At point B the economy is in stock equilibrium. At that

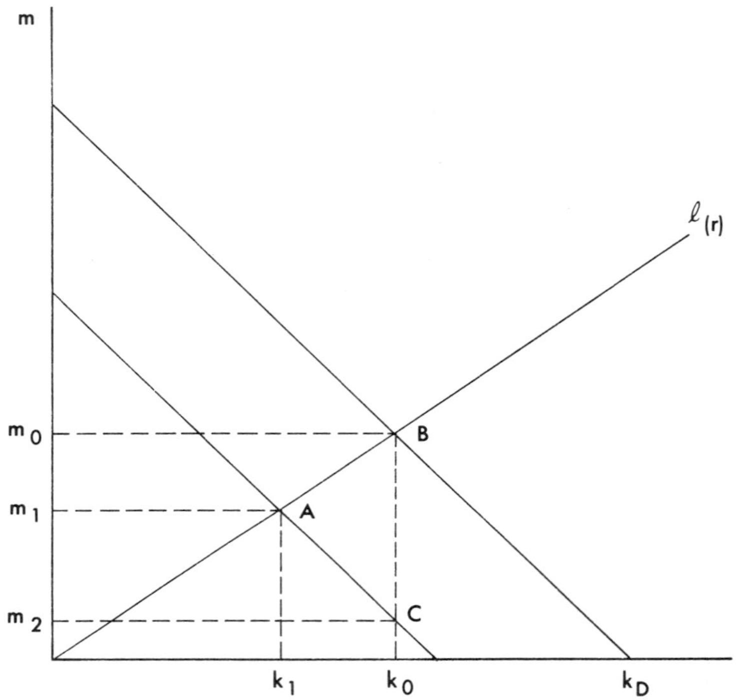

Figure 2: The adjustment path to devaluation in the portfolio model.

point expenditure equals income, and real balances m_0 and shares of equity k_0 are held in the ratio desired at interest rate r. Devaluation, however, disturbs the equilibrium. While equity holdings remain at k_0, real balances fall to m_2 at point C. The economy now is on a lower real wealth constraint and the actual ratio of real balances to equity deviates from the desired ratio. Portfolios are assumed to adjust to the desired ratio instantaneously. So the observed impact effect will be a movement from point C to point A. At point A the economy has a current account surplus, so assets will accumulate along the ray $\ell(r)$ until point B is again reached.

The effect of devaluation is to produce a temporary current account surplus until the reduction in real assets caused by devaluation can be offset. Notice that if the government had accompanied the devaluation with a proportional increase in the nominal money supply, the economy would move directly back from point C to point B. In other words, devaluation would have no real effect.

The Dornbusch model implies a similar result. Initial equilibrium in the model is at interest rate r_o and real asset holdings (other than the nontraded capital) v_0. At that combination of real tradable assets and interest rates, the existing stock of nontradable capital will just be demanded (as shown by the kk curve in Figure 3b) and savings just equals investment (as shown in Figure 3a).

Devaluation, unaccompanied by a proportionate increase in the money supply, reduces the real value of tradable assets from v_o to v_1. As wealth falls, the demand for nontradable capital falls. In order to convince domestic investors to hold the existing supply of domestic capital, the rate of return must rise to r_1. The rise in the rate of return makes the domestic capital more attractive and reduces the value of the stock to be held. Also, since the ratio of money to equity has fallen, portfolio holdings must be returned to the desired ratio. This portfolio adjustment is assumed to occur immediately.

The lower value of traded assets v_1 has reduced the level of real wealth. The reduction of real wealth shifts the savings curve in Figure 3a down. The rate of return on domestic capital has risen to r_1. The domestic rate of savings has clearly risen while the level of investment has fallen. The country now has a current account surplus. The division of the surplus between tradable equity and money will be determined by the interest rate on traded equities, just as in the Frenkel-Rodriguez model. In fact all the implications of the Dornbusch model are the same

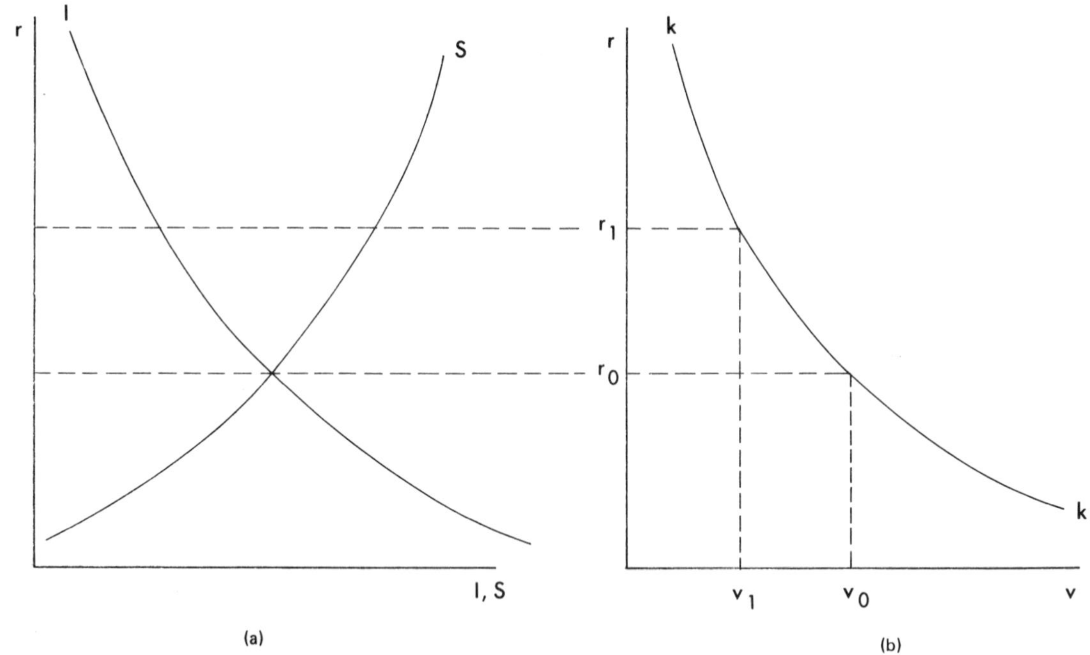

Figure 3: The portfolio model when nontraded assets exist, of which (a) shows the level of absorption given the rate of return on the nontraded asset, and (b) shows the determination of the rate of return on the nontraded asset given the real value of traded assets.

as the Frenkel-Rodriguez model, except that the temporary rise in the return on domestic capital causes the rate of production of this capital to fall temporarily, and thus some oscillation in the domestic capital stock. Notice that again all real effects of devaluation would disappear if the government increased the money supply to keep the real tradeable asset level at v_0.

The predictions of this type of model on the foreign accounts can be divided into two parts, the impact effect of adjusting the portfolio and the effect of returning real wealth to previous levels. The impact effect will be dominated by the exchange of bonds for money in order to adjust holdings to their desired levels. This implies both initial capital account and balance of payments surpluses. Even if the current account is unchanged, the trade balance must improve. The capital account surplus implies a worsening in the debt service account which must be offset by a trade balance improvement to keep the current account at its original level. To the extent that the current account initially improves, the initial trade balance improvement must be even larger.

The portfolio adjustment impact effect, however, is assumed in these models to occur instantaneously. Therefore, for empirical study the changes in wealth along $\ell(r)$ are more important. Since real wealth has fallen following devaluation, nominal and real expenditure also fall. Assuming a constant level of domestic output, equation (2.5) shows that the trade balance will improve. The previously shown improvement in the current account implies that the balance of payments also improves. The balance of payments surplus will be the constant function $\ell/1+\ell$ of the current account surplus. Over time the current account surpluses will cause the level of the country's real wealth to rise. The rise in wealth raises expenditure. The trade balance and current account, and thus the balance of payments, surpluses will decline towards zero.

CONSTANT NOMINAL PRICE OF THE NONTRADED GOOD

An alternative assumption that produces real effects is to hold the nominal price of one good constant. A convenient good for this purpose is one which is produced and consumed only in the home country. The model of devaluation now contains three goods, importables, exportables and non-traded goods. The relative price of exportables and importables is assumed unchanged.[1] Equation (2.1) now becomes

$$X_i = f(P_i, P_j, P_N, E) \tag{2.9}$$

where P_N is the price of nontraded goods.

A model of this type has been analyzed by Dornbusch (1974a, 1975a). In that model he finds that as long as the terms of trade do not change, the trade balance unequivocally improves. The Dornbusch discussion is in terms of a goods model with only brief reference to monetary policy. But with some minor changes the model converts into one of the goods, money and bonds markets.

Since the nominal quantity that the government wants to hold constant is now the nominal price of home goods, real effects from any other source must be eliminated. Specifically, changes in real wealth must be avoided. As shown in previous sections, changes in real wealth can by themselves produce real effects. Monetary policy will therefore be reintroduced by assuming its purpose is to keep the real value of money balances constant.

Capital transactions will again be in shares of equity. If the small country assumption is made, the

---

1 Constant terms of trade is consistent with a small country assumption. It is also consistent with a two country model with identical marginal propensities to spend and elasticities of substitution.

interest rate on these shares will be given. Notice that since devaluation does not affect the real value of money balances, equities or the interest rate, there will be no instantaneous shifting of portfolios in this model. In the absence of further government actions, portfolios would remain balanced and the current account surplus would be zero.

The immediate effect of devaluation is to raise the price of traded goods. The change in domestic traded goods prices is again

$$\dot{P} = \dot{e} + \dot{P}^* \qquad (2.4)$$

where the "•" refers to percentage changes and the asterisk denotes the foreign country. With the small country assumption $\dot{P}^*=0$ and traded goods' prices rise in domestic currency by the percentage of devaluation.

The rise in the traded goods price puts pressure on the nontraded goods price to rise. Employing Salter's (1959) graph of aggregate domestic supply and demand in Figure 4, the cause of the upward pressure is found. At point A the economy is at "full" equilibrium. Domestic demand just equals supply. Devaluation, however, raises the relative price of tradables. The domestic response is a shift on the production side towards tradables (point B), while demand shifts towards nontradables (point C). In the absence of government action, the nominal price of nontradables will rise until the pre-devaluation relative price has been regained and the economy is again producing and consuming at point A.

The Salter graph must be reinterpreted slightly for this model. Where no capital transactions are assumed, the transformation curve represents total domestic production as well as the country's budget constraint, i.e., GNP as well as GDP. But with the inclusion of capital account transactions, GNP and GDP will now differ by the net service account balance. The service account balance affects the budget constraint for tradables, but not

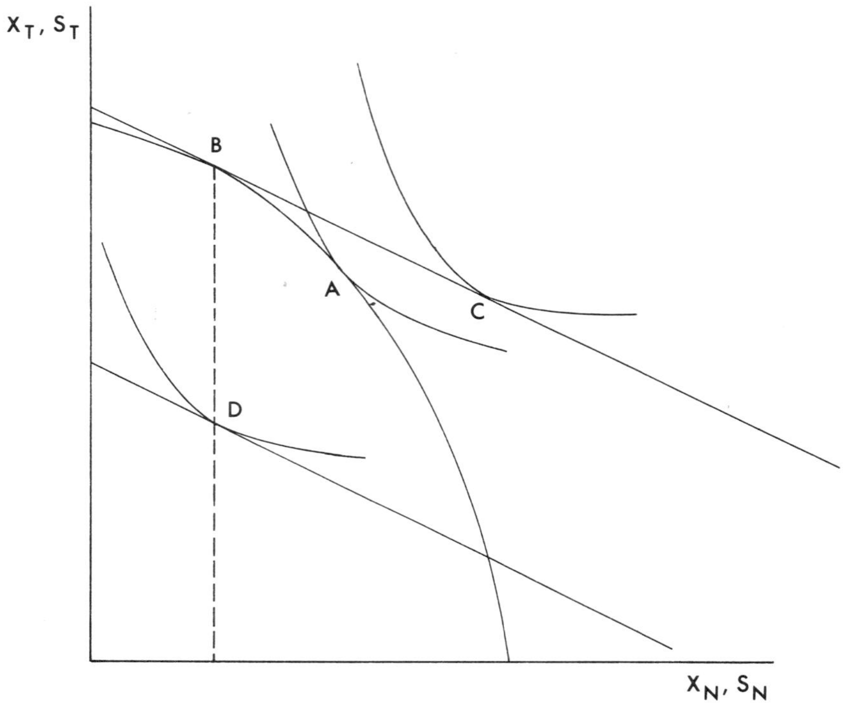

Figure 4: Salter's graph relating demand and supply of traded and nontraded goods.

nontradables. The model can therefore be adjusted by merely redefining the horizontal axis. Rather than always being zero in value, the horizontal axis will equal the service account. Changes in the service account are associated with changes in the level of wealth and thus in the demand for both goods through their wealth elasticities. But since the service flow can only be paid in tradables, changes in the service flow cause changes in the relative supplies and possibly the relative price of nontradables.

In order to prevent the nominal price of nontradables from rising, the government must act to keep supply equal to demand. This equilibrium is accomplished through fiscal policy. When there is excess demand for nontradables, the government reduces expenditure through taxation. In the presence of excess supply, the government subsidizes the private sector until all nontradables are consumed.

In terms of Figure 4 the nontraded goods market clears at point D, where demand has been reduced by D-C in terms of nontradables. The reduced consumption also produces an excess supply of tradables equal to B-D. This quantity is the current account surplus. The current account surplus will be larger the smaller the country's marginal propensity to spend on home goods because expenditure must be reduced by more to eliminate a given excess demand for nontradables. The surplus will also be larger the larger the demand and supply elasticities. The larger these elasticities, the larger the excess demand for nontradables from a given rise in the price of tradables. The current account surplus will again be divided in the proportion $\ell(r)$ between money and equities. The surplus is financed by exporting the excess supply of tradables. Thus the impact effect of devaluation in the model is to improve the trade balance, the balance of payments, and the service account, but to worsen the capital account.

The subsequent paths of the accounts depend on the function $\ell(r)$ and the wealth elasticities of demand. The smaller $\ell(r)$, the greater the proportion of equities imported, implying a larger increase in the domestic supply (budget constraint) of tradables. The smaller the wealth elasticity of demand for tradables, the less demand rises with a given current account surplus. Two possibilities arise. One is that the domestic demand for tradables rises sufficiently faster than supply to allow the economy to come to equilibrium at point B. A second possibility is that the supply of tradables rises faster than demand, initially enlarging the current account surplus. An increased current account surplus implies a larger supply of tradables for the rest of the world at a time that the rest of the world's assets are falling. Such a situation must lead to world excess supply of tradables and therefore a fall in the nominal price. The interest rate may also fall. Final equilibrium will occur in this case closer to point A in Figure 4.

It must be pointed out, however, that the results of this model depend heavily on the assumption of myopic behavior. The most important mechanism in the model is the fiscal policy. Without an effective fiscal policy, the relative price of traded and nontraded goods could not be permanently changed. The effectiveness of the fiscal policy requires that the government reduce real wealth in order to reduce real expenditure. However, any possible reduction in real wealth may depend directly on other assumptions.

Taxation is one form of financing government expenditure. Thus, when the government raises taxes, it is financing a larger proportion of present government expenditures by directly reducing present private expenditures. But because taxation is used to finance present expenditure, issuing of money and bonds can be reduced. If the government is following an optimal policy, a reduction in the present issuing means more can be issued in the future. Issuing more money and bonds in the future means future tax liabilities are reduced. A reduction in future tax liabilities raises present private wealth and causes present private expenditure to rise, offsetting the initial effects of the fiscal policy. Thus only with an assumption of myopic behavior or nonoptimal government policy can the results of this model hold.

INCLUDING THE EFFECTS OF NOMINAL CAPITAL ASSETS

The above models exclude from consideration any international trading in domestic currency denominated assets. Domestic currency is not held in foreign countries. The only internationally traded assets are dollar denominated bonds and equities. Such assets are assumed to retain their real value following devaluation. Goods are also traded in terms of their real values. However, it is also possible that a country is holding a net wealth item which is tied to an international contract denominated in domestic currency. The two obvious cases are internationally traded bonds and import or export contracts. In the following sections the implications of including these domestic currency net wealth items are investigated. It is concluded that these items add a source of real effects in all the models and may therefore change the models' predictions. The necessary conditions for changes in the predictions are then examined.

Domestic Currency-Denominated Bonds Within the Initial Model of Devaluation

The only bonds thus far considered internationally tradable have been bonds denominated in foreign currency. These bonds are considered unaffected by exchange rate changes in the small country models. Devaluation raises the domestic currency price level by the percentage of devaluation. But since the foreign currency bonds also rise in value of terms of domestic currency by the percentage of devaluation, no real change is effected.

Domestic currency-denominated bonds create a different result. Devaluation still raises the domestic price level by the percentage of devaluation, but since the bonds' values are fixed in terms of domestic currency, their real value must fall. Real wealth effects have been created.

One may wonder why faced with a choice between a bond whose real value never changes and one whose real value may change an individual will choose the latter one. The answer lies in the concept of portfolio diversification. An individual may desire to diversify his portfolio to include "risky" assets as well as "riskless" ones. To the extent that individuals perceive a chance of exchange rate changes, the additional risk should appear in an interest rate differential between domestic currency and foreign currency denominated assets.

The analysis will be concerned with only net foreign holdings of domestically denominated bonds. Of course, as previously shown, domestic residents may hold these bonds. But while they are holding an asset, they are simultaneously holding a liability. The real value of both the asset and liability fall following devaluation. While distribution effects may occur, devaluation causes no net bond wealth effect in the domestic country. The possible domestic distribution effects will again be ignored. Market imperfections such as private creditors discounting their future consumption at a different rate than private debtors discount their future liabilities will also be ignored. Similarly, taxpayers are again assumed to perfectly foresee their future tax liabilities and to discount them at the same rate as the government.

When foreigners hold domestic currency bonds the net creditor and debtor position in both countries in terms of domestic currency has changed. The foreign country holds an asset of the domestic country and the domestic country holds the liability. Devaluation will cause net wealth effects in both countries. The foreign country, the net creditor in domestic currency, will find the real value of its assets reduced. The domestic country, the net debtor, will find the real value of its liabilities reduced. The changes in the real value of wealth will cause changes in expenditure in both countries. In the domestic country the level of expenditure will rise relative to income. The country will run a current account deficit. The level of wealth will continue to be reduced until income again equals expenditure. The opposite occurs in the foreign country. Thus including the possibility of domestic currency-denominated bonds brings back the transfer properties of devaluation even if all assets and liabilities are perfectly foreseen and discounted, and if the government follows an optimal policy.

Currency Contracts

As pointed out by Magee (1973) the contracting and delivery of traded goods may not occur simultaneously. There may be several months between the ordering and delivery of these goods. If an unanticipated devaluation should occur during this time, distribution effects again occur between countries. The exact effects depend on the currency in which the contract is denominated.

As with the bonds, distribution effects occur only if the contract is denominated in domestic currency. But the effects would not occur even then if trade were balanced and all contracts were in domestic currency. Thus, in order to get a distribution effect, the value of export contracts denominated in domestic currency must differ from the value of import contracts similarly denominated. If export contracts are larger than import contracts, devaluation will produce a net loss of wealth for the country. The loss in wealth from a reduction in the real value of payments for the country's exports will outweigh the gain from the reduction in the real value of payments for imports. If the value of domestic currency contracts for imports is greater than for exports, the country will have an increase in wealth. There is again a transfer of wealth which will produce a temporary change in the current account.

It is important to simultaneously consider the bond and goods contract effects since they are often financially related. Domestic currency bonds represent a method for traders to take a covered position in foreign transactions. For example, suppose a foreign country trader contracts in domestic currency for the delivery of goods in ninety days. In order to avoid possible currency exchange risk over the ninety day period, he may decide to simultaneously buy ninety day, domestic currency-denominated bonds in the amount of the contract. He is then assured of having the required amount of domestic currency at the rate at which he originally contracted. During the ninety day period he is both a net debtor and creditor in domestic currency. If an unanticipated devaluation occurs, the real loss in value of this bond holdings is just offset by the real gain in value of his currency contract.

Similarly, if the foreigner expects to deliver goods in ninety days at a fixed domestic currency price, he may become a net debtor in domestic currency bonds for ninety days. He issues a domestic currency-denominated bond at the same time that he negotiates the goods contract. The proceeds of the bond issuance can then be immediately converted into the foreign currency. The trader then has an export contract and a bond liability in equivalent amounts that mature simultaneously. Again, the exchange risk has been arbitraged by simultaneously being both a creditor and debtor in foreign currency.

Because the bond and goods contracts may be used together, one must not examine them separately to search for the effects of devaluation. Rather one should examine the net position of the country after the value of the two types of contracts have been combined. Thus the bond and goods contracts are important only to the extent that the net creditor position in goods (net import contracts) differs from the net debtor position in domestic currency bonds.

Including the Bond and Currency Contract Effects in the Portfolio Model of Devaluation

The portfolio model described in a previous section can be adjusted slightly to incorporate the effects of bond and currency contracts in domestic currency. The primary

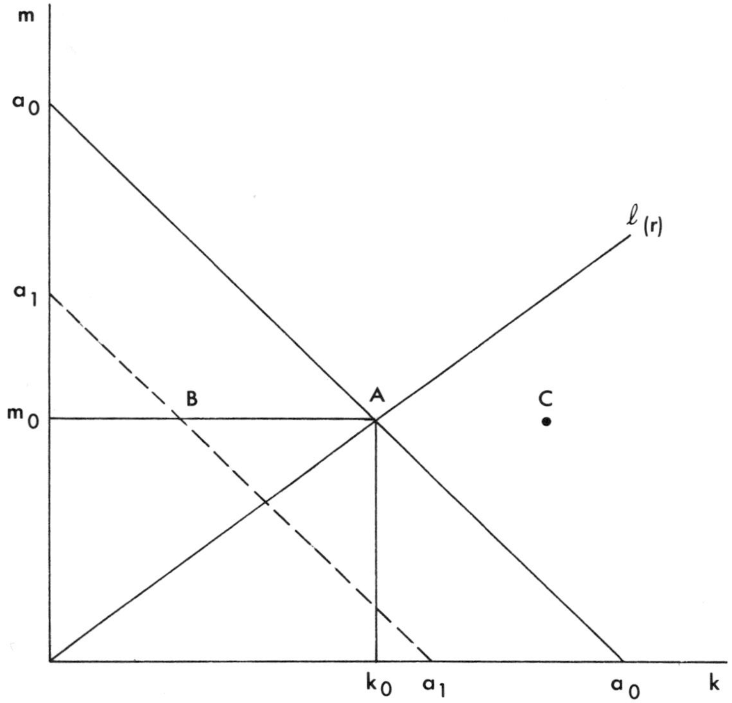

Figure 5: The effects of devaluation in the portfolio model when nominal bonds and currency contracts are included.

change is to add the net international debtor or creditor position in domestic currency to the net holdings of other assets. The vertical axis of Figure 5 still represents real money balances. The horizontal axis, however, has now a slightly broader interpretation. The real value of the capital holdings k is computed as the sum of all net domestic investments plus net foreign investment. The foreign investment may still take the form of shares of equities. But they may also take the form of domestic currency-denominated contracts. The nominally-denominated contracts provide additional potential wealth effects.

In Figure 5 the country is in a stationary state at wealth level a_o, shown by wealth constraint $a_o a_o$. At that

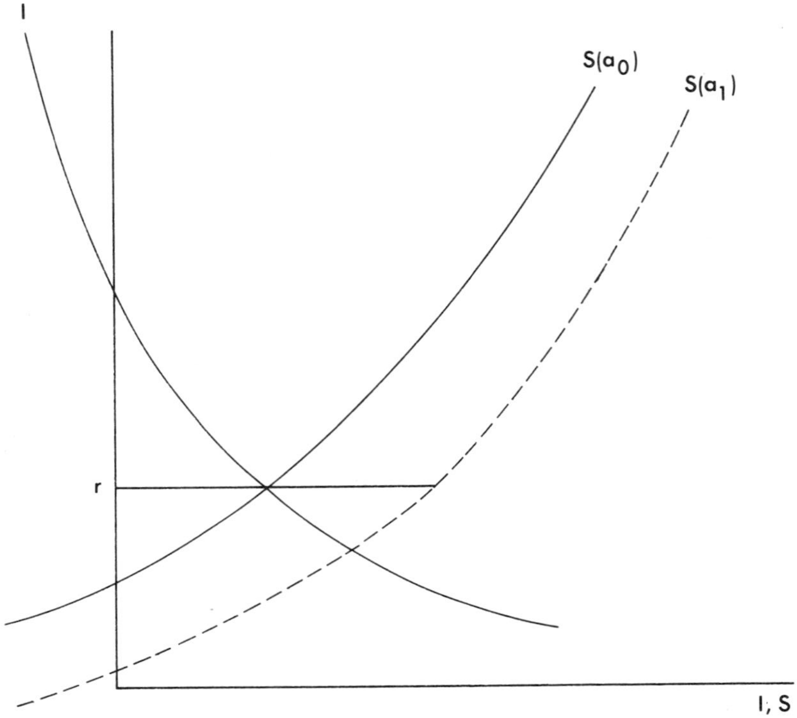

Figure 6: The effects of devaluation on net absorption.

level of wealth, income (GNP) is just equal to expenditure, so there is no tendency for wealth to change. Investment, however, may still be positive, depending on the rate of depreciation. With a positive rate of depreciation, the rate of investment must equal the rate of depreciation in order to maintain the stationary state. A positive rate of depreciation is assumed in Figure 6. At the stationary state, equilibrium associated with wealth level a_o, savings equals investment. The savings and investment curves, however, intersect at a positive value. Positive rates of investment must occur in order to keep the level of wealth constant.

Devaluation affects the country by changing the level and composition of wealth. Real money balances are reduced as long as the government does not increase the nominal quantity by the percentage of devaluation. The portion of net contracts denominated in domestic currency is also affected. As previously stated, real contract values increase if the country is a net debtor and decrease if a net creditor. The shift in the wealth constraint will be determined by the sum of the two wealth effects. If the country is a net creditor in nominal contracts, real wealth clearly falls. But if the country is a net debtor, the level of real wealth may be unchanged or even rise. The savings curve in Figure 6 shifts with wealth, causing at world interest rate r a current account surplus or deficit as wealth falls or rises. The effects on the other accounts are analyzed below.

Case #1--The Monetary Authority Offsets the Change in Real Balances. Assume that the monetary authorities of the domestic country follow a policy of keeping the real money supply constant. The only real effect is from the nominal contracts. If the country is a net creditor in contracts, it will move from point A to point B in Figure 5. Real wealth has been reduced to a_1. The impact effect of devaluation causes the country to run balance of payments and capital account deficits in order to bring the portfolio back into equilibrium along ray $\ell(r)$. A capital account deficit with a constant current account implies a permanent worsening in the trade account.

However, the current account does not remain constant. The reduced level of wealth will reduce actual wealth below the desired level, causing a greater rate of savings at every interest rate. The savings curve shifts to the right. Thus once portfolios are again balanced along $\ell(r)$, the country will run a balance of payments and current account surplus and a capital account deficit.

The current account surplus will be associated with an improvement in the trade balance. This improvement must be larger than the deterioration caused by the impact effect. As the country moves along $\ell(r)$ towards point A, the current account surplus is reduced and the capital account is continuously in deficit. Both effects cause the trade balance to deteriorate. Yet at point A the real value of the trade balance must be the same as before devaluation.[2] The trade balance must therefore have a net surplus as $\ell(r)$ is reached.

If the country is a net debtor, real liabilities are reduced. The country will find itself at point C in Figure 5. The impact effect is a surplus on the balance of payments and on the capital account. The trade balance improves. But since the real level of wealth has increased, the ensuing adjustment period will be characterized by current and money account deficits and a capital account surplus. The trade balance initially improves, shows a net deterioration once $\ell(r)$ is reached, and returns to its predevaluation level as point A is reapproached.

Thus the contract effect by itself tends to cause the initial balance of payments surplus and trade account deficit to switch signs over the period of adjustment and causes the capital and current account surpluses to retain the same sign.

Case #2--A Creditor Country With Constant Nominal Money Supplies. If the monetary authorities do not intervene to keep the real money supply constant, the real value of the money supply is reduced by devaluation. The reduction in real balances combined with the net foreign creditor position of the country implies that the country's wealth is

---

[2] Notice, however, that if devaluation raises the nominal price of tradables, a constant real trade deficit implies a larger nominal trade deficit.

clearly reduced. The country will be at some point D to the southwest of point A in Figure 5. The only remaining question is whether point D will be to the right or the left of the $\ell(r)$ line. The position of point D will be determined by the initial ratio of money balances to nominally denominated bonds. The most probable case is that the ratio will exceed the ratio $\ell(r)$. At point A all money is nominally denominated, but not all capital assets. Devaluation will therefore reduce the real value of money more than the real value of bonds. Point D will lie to the right of $\ell(r)$. The adjustment of the accounts will be just like in the case where only real balances are reduced. In fact the case with only reduced real balances is simply an extreme example of the present case, i.e., no net contracts in domestic currency. The impact effect will be surpluses on the monetary and capital accounts and an improvement in the trade balance. Following the impact effect, the current account will be in surplus as money and bonds are reaccumulated. The trade balance also is in surplus. As the economy moves up $\ell(r)$ to the original level of wealth, the current, monetary and trade accounts become increasingly less positive, and the capital account less negative.

It is at least theoretically possible that the initial ratio of money balances to nominal bonds is less than $\ell(r)$. The measure along the horizontal axis in Figure 5 is the <u>net</u> holdings of capital assets. But suppose that the initial holdings of assets k_o are composed of k_o+k_1 net contracts denominated in domestic currency, k_2 of liabilities denominated in foreign currency and k_3 of real claims of foreigners on domestic capital. If $k_1=|k_2+k_3|$ then initial net capital assets are k_o. However, since

$$\frac{m_o}{k_o} > \frac{m_o}{k_o + k_1}$$

devaluation reduces the real value of the contracts more than real balances. Point D lies to the left of $\ell(r)$ and the analysis is the same as for Case #1.

Case #3--A Debtor Country With Fixed Nominal Money Supply-A. The net debtor position of the country means that the real value of the contracts are increased by devaluation. However, in most cases the reduction in real balances will still outweigh the increase in wealth. Total real wealth declines. This case is shown in Figure 7.

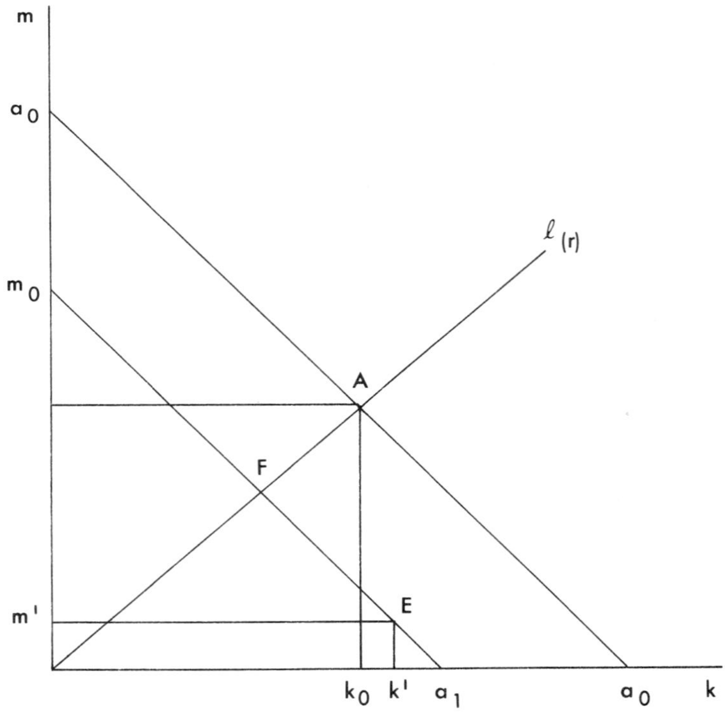

Figure 7: The effects of devaluation when the negative real balance effect still outweighs the reduction in real liabilities.

The initial holdings of the country are still m_o real money balances and k_o real capital assets. Devaluation reduces real balances to m' and increases capital assets to k'. The economy moves to point E. Portfolio adjustment requires the country to move immediately to point F. Over time the economy will move back to point A. Notice that the initial current account surplus should be smaller here than in Case #2. For any given reduction in real balances, the country will be on a higher wealth constraint the greater the net value of its capital assets. Case #2 represents situations to the left of the Ak_o line in Figure 7. Case #3 represents those cases to the right of the line. Thus Case #3 represents larger values of net capital assets. The positive wealth effect in the capital asset market has caused a smaller reduction in wealth for any real balance effect. The current account surplus at point F must be smaller, as must the capital account deficit and balance of payments and trade account surpluses. Devaluation has a smaller net effect on the foreign accounts.

Case #4: A Debtor Country With Fixed Nominal Money Supply-B. If the ratio of money to nominal contracts in less than m_o/k_o, then, as discussed in Case #2, the effect of devaluation in the bond market must be larger than the real balance effect. Since the wealth effect in the bond market is positive, the overall level of wealth rises in this case.

The increase in the level of wealth shifts the wealth constraint from a_oa_o to a_2a_2 in Figure 8. After the portfolio has returned to equilibrium at point G, the current account will be in deficit.

To arrive at point G, the impact effect must involve balance of payments and capital account surpluses. Since devaluation reduces real balances and increases capital,

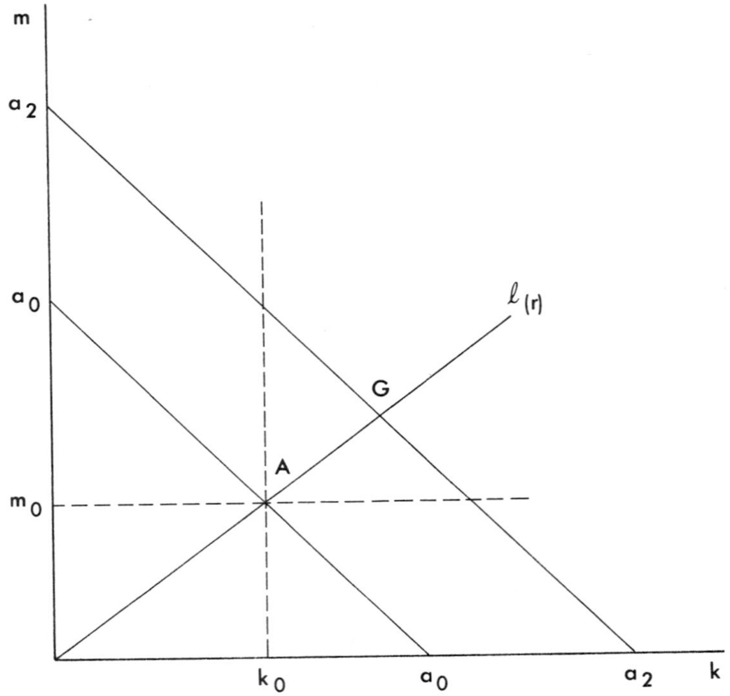

Figure 8: The effects of devaluation when the reduction in real liabilities increases real net wealth.

the country must be at some point M southeast of A. Since the increase in bond wealth is greater than the reduction in real balances, the point M will be to the right of both the $a_o a_o$ and $\ell(r)$ lines. Such a point represents excess supply of bonds and excess demand for money, hence the capital and monetary account surpluses.

The impact effect also has the effect of improving the trade account. However, after point G is reached, the economy will be running current account and balance of payments deficits, and a capital account surplus. The trade balance will show a net deterioration from the initial position. This deterioration will disappear as point A is reapproached.

SUMMARY AND EMPIRICAL IMPLICATIONS

The major differences in the models described above are whether the public is assumed to perfectly discount its future assets and liabilities and whether the government is assumed to follow an optimal monetary policy. If perfect discounting and optimal government policy are assumed, the government is no longer able to affect real variables like the trade balance. Monetary policy will offset only the balance of payments and capital accounts. Increasing the money supply is like an open market purchase. The public's holdings of money increase while net holdings of bonds decrease. Only a portfolio adjustment is necessary, and the adjustment is accomplished through a joint balance of payments and capital account surplus. Similarly fiscal policy is ineffective in affecting the trade balance because it too cannot affect real wealth. Increasing taxation reduces present wealth, but increases future wealth by an equivalent amount. Expenditure is unaffected. In such a model it is not surprising that devaluation has no effect on the trade balance. Devaluation causes the domestic price level to rise. But because there are assumed to be no domestic currency-denominated net assets, no real wealth effects occur. Devaluation, like monetary policy, only causes private portfolios to deviate from their desired ratio of money to bonds. The only effect is a portfolio adjustment.

The alternative model presented above does not assume the public to accurately foresee and discount all future assets and liabilities, nor that the government is following an optimal monetary policy. In this model both monetary and fiscal policy have real effects. Because money is viewed as a net asset, changing the money supply changes real wealth. Because increased taxation is viewed as reducing present wealth, but not increasing future wealth, fiscal policy can also affect real expenditure. In such a model devaluation alone will produce temporary real effects. The rising price level reduces the real wealth value of the money supply. Until this loss of wealth is reaccumulated through current account surpluses, expenditure will be reduced and the trade balance should show a surplus. Of course this temporary affect may be prolonged through appropriate government policy.

These two models provide several specific conclusions that can be tested empirically. First, if money is not net wealth, monetary policy should have little affect on the trade balance. The trade balance will change only if real effects occur. Monetary policy can therefore affect the trade balance only to the extent that real balances are increased. Similarly, if fiscal policy has no wealth effect, changes in the trade balance should be unrelated to changes in fiscal policy. Devaluation will therefore be unrelated to changes in the trade balance. Because devaluation is equivalent to a decrease in the nominal money supply, where money is not net wealth, real wealth and the trade balance are unaffected. On the other hand, if policy actions have wealth effects, as assumed in the portfolio model, devaluation should temporarily improve the trade balance.

For the balance of payments, however, the predictions do not diverge. Both models predict temporary improvements in the balance of payments. If money is net wealth, the balance of payments improves because wealth is reaccumulated at the ratio $\ell(r)$ between money and bonds. If money is not net wealth, readjustment of portfolios require importation of money. The net wealth model is therefore consistent with improvements in both the trade account and balance of payments. The other model, however, is consistent with only the balance of payments improving. The trade account deficit should be unchanged in real terms, or become more negative in nominal terms due to the effect of increased prices.

The only remaining factor to account for is the net value of foreign bonds and contracts denominated in domestic currency. Changes in the real value of these assets can produce real effects even when no other source of real effects exists. If data were available showing contract denominations, these effects could be tested.

Empirical tests of these models are described in Chapters IV-VI. The empirical models employed attempt to measure the different effects suggested in this chapter. From the tests it is hoped to conclude whether devaluation affects the balance of payments and/or the trade balance, and thus which model is more consistent with past behavior.

Chapter III

EMPIRICAL STUDIES OF DEVALUATION

Chapter II presents the theoretical framework for analyzing the effects of devaluation. Within this general equilibrium framework the effect of devaluation on the trade balance depends heavily on the net value of fiat money, on whether the government holds some nominal quantity constant, and on the currency in which foreign contracts are denominated. This chapter discusses previous empirical studies of the effects of devaluation. These studies are few in number and limited in scope. However, the studies do provide preliminary indications as to which of the theories presented in Chapter II are more empirically correct. The results from these studies provide a basis of comparison for the more in depth empirical tests of Chapters IV-VI.

The most widely quoted study is by Richard Cooper (1971a, 1971b). The study covers twenty-four devaluations of nineteen developing countries during the period 1959-66. Cooper's emphasis is on the impact effect of devaluation. He examines the one year change in the level of the foreign accounts from the year of devaluation to the following year. In fifteen of the twenty-four cases the balance on goods and services improves in the year following devaluation as compared to the preceding year. However, in ten of these fifteen cases the account is still negative after the improvement. On the other hand, the balance of payments tends not only to improve but also to be positive following devaluation. In seventeen of the twenty-four cases the balance of payments improves. In fourteen of the cases where improvements occur, the balance of payments is in surplus following devaluation. Furthermore, in six of the nine cases where the current account worsens, the balance of payments improves. In other words, the increase in capital flows more than offsets the worsening of the trade balance in these countries.

Cooper's findings on the impact effect of devaluation are consistent with the theories that expect both the current account and the balance of payments to improve. However, there are two shortcomings to Cooper's approach. First, levels of the foreign accounts are not reported for additional years. Thus there is no basis to compare the "improved" level of the account with pre-devaluation levels. Does the improvement compensate for any deterioration caused by devaluation? Furthermore, by failing to report results for additional years after devaluation, it is impossible to determine if the improvement is temporary or permanent.

A second problem with his analysis is that additional policy variables are not accounted for. For example, the Monetary Approach to the balance of payments predicts that, all other things held constant, devaluation should cause a temporary surplus in the balance of payments. But typically all other things are not held constant. Specifically, changes in government policies such as the rate of domestic credit creation often accompany devaluation. The Monetary Approach predicts that these policies can also have sizable effects on the balance of payments. In order to accurately measure the effects of just devaluation, the effects of the additional policies must be incorporated into the analysis. Failure to account for the other effects is equivalent to ascribing all changes in the accounts to devaluation. However, despite these limitations of the analysis, Cooper's results provide an initial indication of the effects of devaluation.

Connolly and Taylor (1972) try to overcome some of the short-comings of the Cooper paper. Using sixteen of the devaluations in the Cooper sample they try to relate improvements in the balance of payments and rates of domestic credit creation. For the sample as a whole they find that the rate of domestic credit creation is on average fourteen percent in the year prior to devaluation. In that year the average foreign reserve loss of these countries is thirty-one percent. In the year following devaluation the rate of credit creation is approximately the same as before, but the countries have an average gain of forty-two percent in reserves. So devaluation improves the rate of foreign reserve accumulation. However, within four to eight quarters following devaluation the average rate of domestic credit creation rises to twenty-nine percent. During this period the rate of reserve accumulation falls to nineteen percent. So most of the improvement occurs within the first year following devaluation, the rate of domestic credit creation possibly accounting for the fall-off in the second year.

Regressions are run relating for all sixteen countries the percentage change in the net foreign reserves of the central bank in the year after devaluation to the rate of devaluation and the rate of the domestic credit creation in the year following devaluation. Connolly and Taylor find: 1.) the higher the rate of devaluation, the greater the improvement in the reserve position, and 2.) the higher the rate of domestic credit expansion following devaluation, the smaller the improvement.

While this study tries to overcome some of the problems of the Cooper study, it does not entirely succeed. The major implications of the study still concern the impact effect of devaluation. In addition there still has been no standardization for other policy variables. The analysis implicitly assumes that the balance of payments would remain unchanged in the absence of devaluation.

Other studies of devaluation have concentrated less on the impact effects and more on whether devaluation improves the trade balance over a period of several years. Laffer (1973) performs one such test for fifteen post-war devaluations. Laffer examines the time path of the trade balance over seven years, from three years before devaluation until three years after. The trade balance is defined in these tests as the level of f.o.b. exports minus the level of c.i.f. imports, both in domestic currency. The purpose of the tests is to determine if trade balances are on average more or less negative in the years following devaluation than in the preceding years. But Laffer has also not accounted for variables other than devaluation. No measure of domestic policy is included. Only the gross association between the time path of the trade balance and the changes in the exchange rate is examined.

The results provide little evidence of devaluation causing significant or sustained improvement in the trade balance. In eight of the fifteen countries the trade balance is more positive or less negative in the year following devaluation than in the year of devaluation. However, any improvement tends to be short-lived. Of the eight countries which show improvements, four have the largest deficits of the seven year period in the three years following devaluation. Furthermore, two of the eight countries which exhibit an improvement do so only because both suffered the worst deficit of the seven years in the year of devaluation. The "improvement" merely returns the trade balance to its pre-devaluation deficit level.

Examining the entire fifteen country sample, Laffer finds that the trade balance on average tends to worsen. Ten of the fifteen countries have the largest deficit of the seven year period in the three years following devaluation. Two more have the largest deficit in the year of devaluation. Ten out of the fourteen countries with data for the third year following devaluation have a larger deficit in that year than in the year after devaluation. Eight of the fourteen have larger deficits two years after than one year after devaluation. There is little evidence of devaluation improving the trade balance.

Laffer's results are reexamined and expanded by Salant (1975). Salant continues to define the trade balance as the difference between f.o.b. exports and c.i.f. imports, but his data are measured in foreign currency (dollars) rather than in domestic currency. This shift to foreign currency causes a slight increase in the frequency of trade balance improvement but the results are still consistent with Laffer's findings. Salant also extends the analysis to the balance of payments. The balance of payments is defined as the change in international reserves minus allocations of SDR's. He finds that devaluation improves the balance of payments in most cases, with the improvement in the combined capital account and non-trade current account more than offsetting any deterioration in the trade balance.

Salant tests the effect of devaluation by summing the levels of the accounts in the three year periods before and after devaluation. These sums are then compared to determine if the average level of the account improves following devaluation. Examining first Laffer's sample of fifteen countries, Salant finds that only eight of the fifteen countries show improvements following devaluation. If the domestic currency value of the trade balance is used, as in Laffer's test, only six of the fifteen countries show improvements. On the other hand, the balance of payments improves in thirteen of the fifteen countries. So while the balance of payments appears to improve on average following devaluation there is no such evidence for the trade balance.

It is interesting to note that in the two cases where the balance of payments worsens the trade balance also worsens. In one such case, Israel 1967, one would expect this result. In 1967 Israel was preparing for and engaging in war. The other case is Denmark 1967.

Salant expands his analysis to a much larger sample of countries. The results of the expanded analysis can be seen in Table 1. First he examines seventy-eight devaluations in less developed countries. In only thirty-eight of these cases does the trade balance improve. In thirty-nine cases the trade balance worsens, and in one case it is unchanged. So the trade balance improves in only one-half the cases. The balance of payments, however, improves in over two-thirds of the cases. After fifty-five devaluations the balance of payments improves while in twenty-three cases it worsens.

TABLE 1
Results of Salant's Analysis

	Trade Balance			Balance of Payments	
	Improve (+)	Worsen (-)	Unchanged (0)	Improve (+)	Worsen (-)
Less developed (78)	38	39	1	55	23
Developed (23)	8	15	0	20	3
Total (101)	46	54	1	75	26

Next Salant examines twenty-three devaluations by developed countries. The results in this sample are even more striking. In only eight cases does the trade balance improve, while in fifteen cases the trade balance worsens. The trade balance improves only about one-third of the time. The balance of payments, however, improves in over 85 percent of the cases, i.e., twenty out of twenty-three.

Putting the two groups together, there are 101 devaluations. The balance of payments improves in about three-quarters of the cases (75 out of 101), while the trade balance improves in less than one-half the cases (46 out of 101). Devaluation clearly improves the balance of payments, but does not seem to affect the trade balance in any particular direction. The results are consistent with theories that expect the balance of payments to improve, but expect little effect on the trade balance. Of course, one must still caution that the test has not taken into account the effects of other domestic policies.

The preceding tests each used yearly data. In an earlier paper Miles (1974a) performs similar tests on quarterly data. Rather than examining the level of the trade balance, however, the behavior of the ratio of exports to imports X/M is examined. The ratio is a measure of the real rather than the nominal trade balance. If devaluation causes the price of tradables to rise, then the absolute value of the nominal trade balance will rise since $TB = P \cdot X - P \cdot M$. With P, the prices of tradables, rising by a given percentage, nominal deficits will become more negative and surpluses more positive. However, $(P \cdot X)/(P \cdot M)$ will be unaffected by the price change. Therefore, if it is assumed that most countries that devalue have trade balance deficits, the measure X/M has a positive bias, i.e., it overestimates any improvement in the trade balance.

Values of X/M are computed for twelve quarters before and twelve quarters after devaluation for seventeen countries. Average values of X/M are computed for each twelve quarter interval. The test is then to determine if the average value of X/M increases following devaluation. The first test is a simple directional test. In eleven of the seventeen countries the average value of X/M is higher following devaluation than preceding it. However, it is not only the direction, but also the magnitude of any change that is important. A difference of the means test is performed to determine if the average value of X/M before devaluation is statistically different from the average X/M after devaluation. In only three of the seventeen countries do the average values differ at the 95 percent level, and in only a total of four countries at the 90 percent level. Next a comparison sample is constructed. The comparison sample consists of two sequential twelve quarter periods for the devaluing countries in time intervals during which no devaluation took place. From these comparison statistics it can be determined if the behavior of the accounts following devaluation differs from the behavior at other times. The statistics are available for only fourteen of the seventeen countries. But of these fourteen non-devaluation cases, in four the average values of X/M are statistically different at the 95 percent level, and a total of six at the 90 percent level, a higher frequency than for the devaluation sample. So devaluation does not cause exports to increase relative to imports at a faster rate than occurs in non-devaluation periods.

The trade balance data may contain a trend since for an undetermined reason the trade balance may be deteriorating or improving over time. The existence of such a trend is accounted for by performing the same difference of the means test on the first differences of the mean. The first differences in the devaluing and non-devaluing samples are compared to determine if they are statistically different. For example, has devaluation caused less deterioration than expected? In only one country do the first differences differ at the 95 percent level, and in only one more country do they differ at the 90 percent level. So even removing a possible trend does not provide evidence of devaluation causing a systematic change.

These tests are repeated for the four quarter intervals immediately preceding and following devaluation. Examining four quarter intervals searches for possible short-run improvements. A short-run improvement could exist, yet be offset and not appear in the twelve quarter tests. In twelve of the seventeen countries the four quarter average value of X/M is higher after devaluation than before. Yet none of these changes is significant at the 95 percent level and only two at the 90 percent level. In the comparison sample, two are significantly different at the 95 percent level. Employing the difference of the means test on the first differences yields no statistically significant values at either the 95 percent or 90 percent levels. So while there is some evidence of positive short-run effects, these effects are statistically very weak.

A similar form of analysis is performed on the balance of payments. Instead of examining the nominal level of the account, a ratio is used. In this case the ratio is the balance of payments to a measure to GNP, i.e., BP/Y. The average value of this ratio in the twelve quarters preceding devaluation is compared to the average value in the twelve quarters following devaluation. In nine of the eleven countries in the devaluation sample, the average level of BP/Y increases following devaluation. In the comparison sample only two of nine countries have improvements. The results are consistent with devaluation causing an improvement in the balance of payments. The magnitude test, however, provides different results. The average levels of BP/Y differ at the 95 percent level in only one country. This result is not very different from the comparison sample where the average values differ in one country at the 90 percent level.

While the magnitude test on the levels is not consistent with devaluation having a significant effect on the balances of payments, the magnitude test on the first differences is. Recall that the test on the first differences standardizes for possible trends. There are seven countries in which the difference of the means test is performed on the first differences. In one country the differences are significant at the 95 percent level. In three countries they differ at the 90 percent level. Thus in four of seven countries devaluation significantly improves the balance of payments relative to the trend.

The implications of these studies is that there is considerably more evidence of the balance of payments improving following devaluation than of the trade balance. Cooper has evidence of a positive impact effect on the trade balance. Laffer's study also evidences improvement in the year following devaluation. But the improvement usually follows a worsening of the trade balance in the year of devaluation, and tends to be more than offset in subsequent years. Miles does not find evidence of even a short run improvement. While the evidence of an improvement of the trade balance is weak, the studies by Connolly and Taylor, Salant and Miles all find evidence of the balance of payments improving in the three years following devaluation.

Again, it should be cautioned that these studies do not account for exogenous variables such as government policy. In order to properly isolate just the effect of devaluation, these variables must be taken into consideration. Devising a method of standardizing for these exogenous variables is the subject of the next chapter.

Chapter IV

TESTING THE TRADE BALANCE AND BALANCE OF PAYMENTS EQUATIONS

As shown in Chapter III, previous analyses of the effects of devaluation on the trade balance and balance of payments have dealt with the raw account figures. Only the improvement or worsening of these numbers following devaluation are reported. Such an approach is equivalent to ascribing all the changes in the accounts to devaluation. No attempt is made to eliminate or standardize for the changes due to other variables. However, devaluation is often accompanied by changes in other government policies such as monetary, government consumption and commercial policy. This chapter describes the methods and variables used for standardizing for these policies and provides empirical verification of the approach.

THE TRADE BALANCE

An absorption model is used for estimating the trade balance. According to the absorption approach

$$TB = Y - E \,, \tag{4.1}$$

where TB is the trade balance, Y is the level of domestic output and E is the level of domestic expenditure. The equation states simply that if domestic expenditure exceeds domestic output, the excess expenditure must come from abroad, i.e., the trade balance will be negative. Alternatively, if the country's expenditure is less than its output, the surplus goods can be exchanged abroad for money and/or bonds. Taking the level of output to be given, the empirical task is to identify those variables which affect the level of expenditure.

The trade balance as measured from January 1 to December 31 is the total (net) inflow or outflow of goods during the calendar year. The total flow also represents the average rate at which goods are flowing net into or out of the country. The other variables in the equation must therefore be of the proper dimensions to relate to the average flow of goods.

The Money Supply

As shown in Chapter II, the effect of the money supply on expenditure will depend on whether the creation of money is viewed as net wealth. If viewed as net wealth, increasing the money supply will increase the level of wealth and therefore the level of expenditure. Increases in the money supply will be associated with deteriorations in the trade balance. However, if the government is seen as simultaneously issuing both a money asset and a liability, wealth is not increased. Increases in the money supply will have little if any effect on the trade balance. Adjustments to increases in the money supply will occur primarily through a worsening of the capital account and balance of payments. So including the money supply variable provides a test of the alternative hypotheses.

Since the variable being standardized for is domestic monetary policy, it is important that the monetary variable reflect only government actions. A measure of domestic credit creation is needed. This requirement eliminates the usual money supply variables such as M1 or

M2 as candidates. M1 (and M2) represents the net result of the actions of the public and banks in addition to those of the government. Banks can influence M1 through their holdings of excess reserves. The public can affect M1 through its desired holdings of currency relative to bank deposits or its division of deposits between demand and time deposits. They can also directly affect high-powered money through the balance of payments. Excess demands for money can be eliminated by exporting bonds and/or goods abroad and importing money through the balance of payments. The government affects M1 through its power to regulate deposit reserve requirements and the domestic credit portion of high-powered money. The ideal monetary variable should therefore incorporate these two powers.

The monetary policy variable actually employed measures only the second of the powers, the control of the domestic portion of high-powered money. Since the trade balance should represent the average flow of goods, the trade balance should be related to the average level of domestic high-powered money over the year. If money is wealth, the higher the average level of money balances the higher the average rate of expenditure and, given the average rate of income, the larger the trade deficit.

Total high-powered money is measured as the level of currency held by the public plus reserves of banks plus foreign reserves. The domestic portion of high-powered money should include only the first two components. So to measure the average level of the domestic portion of high-powered money, one-half the changes in currency and bank reserves during the year is added to the level of currency plus bank reserves at the beginning of the year. However, since a measure of only domestic monetary policy is desired, changes in reserves or currency due to external sources must be excluded. Thus the balances of payments is subtracted from the changes before being added to the initial level of high-powered money. Subtracting the balance of payments eliminates changes in high-powered money due to domestic residence selling goods or bonds abroad and converting the foreign currency into domestic currency.

One might argue that using high-powered money underestimates the effect of the domestic monetary authorities since the currency created has a multiple effect through the money multiplier. However, since the public's ability to eliminate excess money balances through the foreign accounts is being measured, high-powered money is the proper variable. For example, suppose a country, initially at stock equilibrium, has a money multiplier of five. If the government increases the level of high-powered money by one dollar, ceteris paribus the country will have an excess supply of money of five dollars. The excess supply may be eliminated by running a balance of payments deficit. But since deficits or surpluses are paid in foreign reserves, which are part of high-powered money, the country will have to run only a one dollar not a five dollar deficit. A one dollar increase in the domestic portion of high-powered money will be associated with a one dollar worsening in the balance of payments.

Government Consumption

Government consumption represents one source of direct expenditure in the economy. Thus, if the government increases the level of its consumption by a dollar, with the level of output constant, the trade balance should worsen by one dollar. The level of government consumption measured during the year represents the average rate at which the government consumes. The measured government consumption can therefore be related directly to the measured trade balance.

Some empirical studies of domestic economies have discovered evidence of a "crowding out" effect, i.e., government consumption merely replacing private consumption (see particularly Laffer and Ranson, 1971, Andersen and Jordan, 1968). If the crowding out occurred instantaneously, government consumption would be expected to have little effect on the trade balance. As government consumption rose, private consumption would fall, leaving total consumption unchanged. However, these studies indicate that it requires three to four quarters for the crowding out to be completed. If the rate of government consumption is raised temporarily during the year, while the actual total rates of consumption in the economy may not differ at the beginning and end of the year, the average rate will rise. The rise in the average rate reflects that period during which the fall in private consumption has not completely offset the rise in government consumption.

Commercial Policy

The primary forms of commercial policy are tariffs and quotas. Tariffs, by raising relative prices, switch expenditures from imports to domestic importables. Quotas directly limit the quantity of importables brought into the country. While these policies affect the level of trade, they probably do not affect the trade balance. They are therefore excluded from the estimated equations.

Recall from equation (4.1) that the trade balance equals the difference between domestic output and expenditure. Expenditure switching policies like tariffs change the form of expenditure but probably not the level. (The effects of tariffs on real balances is the one possible exception. See Mussa, 1975). Raising tariffs will therefore reduce the level of imports and raise expenditures on domestically produced importables. But unless the rise in tariffs also improves the level of output, the trade balance will not improve. With a constant level of output, increasing expenditure on domestic output means fewer surplus goods which can be sold abroad. The level of exports falls. In fact, if both output and expenditure remain constant, the fall in imports exactly equals the fall in exports. The trade balance is unchanged. A similar analysis holds for quotas. So while changes in tariffs and quotas may be very important for estimating changes in exports and imports, they are much less important for explaining changes in the trade balance. For this reason, and because meaningful aggregate measures of tariffs and quotas are hard to construct, a commercial policy variable is not include in the trade balance equation.

THE BALANCE OF PAYMENTS

The balance of payments must also be standardized for government policy. The primary policy which affects the balance of payments is monetary policy. If money is viewed as net wealth, an increase in the money supply raises the value of real balances. Given the level of income and the interest rate, real balances will now exceed their desired levels. A country can then reduce the level of real balances to its equilibrium level by running a balance of payments deficit. Alternatively, if money is not viewed as net wealth, increasing the money supply is equivalent to simultaneously increasing both money assets and bond liabilities. The ratio of money assets to bond assets has been increased. Given the interest rate and initial equilibrium, a country will want to return the ratio to its original value. The adjustment of the ratio can be accomplished by exchanging money for bonds abroad. In other words the capital account and balance of payments will deteriorate. So an increase in the money supply should be associated with a deterioration of the balance of payments regardless of whether money is viewed as net wealth.

The domestic portion of high-powered money is again used as a measure of monetary policy. Since the balance of payments represents the average rate of inflow or outflow of reserves, the average level of high-powered money is again used. Increases in this stock of money lead to a worsening in the balance of payments.

While monetary policy is very important for explaining the behavior of the balance of payments, neither government consumption nor commercial policy is. Government consumption primarily affects the rate of absorption of goods. To the extent that the policy affects the level of income, the demand for money will be changed and government consumption will have an indirect effect on the balance of payments. This effect, however, would be captured in the growth rate variable discussed below. To the extent that government consumption is financed by printing money there will also be an effect on the balance of payments. This effect, however, is already measured in the monetary policy variable.

The affect of tariffs and quotas is to switch expenditure from foreign to domestic goods. However, as shown above, these policies will affect only the level of trade, not the trade balance. So tariffs and quotas should have little affect on the balance of payments.

One additional foreign account barrier sometimes imposed is capital controls. Capital controls attempt to reduce the outflow of capital and thus improve the balance of payments. Such reasoning, however, reflects a partial equilibrium analysis. The capital account is simultaneously composed of both inflows and outflows of capital. The measured capital account is the net of the two flows. The net figure represents a country's desired accumulation or decumulation of money through the capital account. Capital controls restrict the outflow of capital. However, they have no direct influence over capital inflows. Given the desired decumulation of money through the capital account, restricting the outflow of money will cause the inflow of adjust. The adjustment of capital inflows to restrictions is shown for short-term capital flows in the U.S. by Laffer (1975b). When the U.S. applied capital controls, the decrease in the capital outflow was just offset by a decrease in the capital inflow. The capital account balance was unchanged from its predicted level. No measure of capital controls is therefore used in the balance of payments equations.

REMAINING ADJUSTMENTS

The levels of the trade balance and balance of payments have thus far been described as merely functions of the levels of domestic variables. However, several problems arise that make this the improper functional form to estimate. These problems are now dealt with.

The first problem is a consequence of regressing non-stationary variables. The trade balance, balance of payments, money variable and government consumption all exhibit time trends. Thus if either the levels or first differences of the variables are used, the values will be observed tc grow over time. Simply regressing the right hand variables on the left hand variable will produce results of little economic significance. The resulting high R^2's will merely indicate that the trends in the independent variables are explaining the trend in the dependent variable.

Circumventing this problem requires changing the functional form. While the levels of TB and Y are both functions of time, the ratio of the two variables probably will not be. The time trend in one variable standardizes for the time trend in the other. The same is true if all other variables are divided by Y. Equation (4.1) becomes

$$TB/Y = 1 - E/Y. \tag{4.1'}$$

The trade balance as a ratio to income is a function of

the expenditure variables (money, government consumption, etc.) to income.

A second problem is whether the estimated equation should be in levels as equation (4.1') or in first differences. As should be clear from the discussion of the policy variables, the function should be in first difference form. Economic theory does not tell us that countries with large money supplies run trade balance or balance of payments deficits. Tastes and preferences for desired cash balances can differ across countries. Rather we expect that it should be countries with large increases in the money supply that find their accounts worsening. Similarly it should be countries with large increases in government consumption that find their trade balances worsening. Equation (4.1') becomes

$$\Delta(TB/Y) = \Delta(E/Y). \tag{4.1''}$$

Changes in the ratio of the trade balance to income are related to changes in the ratio of expenditure to income.

The expenditure variable has thus far been described as a function of merely domestic policies. Economic theory tells us this would be true only if there were no change in other countries' variables, or if other countries' actions did not affect us. However, in a world with essentially fixed exchange rates and substantial trade, actions in one country are certainly expected to be felt in others. (See Lee, 1976 and Laffer, 1975a for empirical verification of this assumption.) Therefore actions in the rest of the world must be taken into account.

In an integrated world goods and money will be expected to flow to wherever excess demand is the greatest. So the analysis of the effects of government policy is concerned not just with whether the policy has raised domestic demand, but if it has raised domestic demand relative to demand in the rest of the world. For example, if the government increases the rate of government consumption, it may raise domestic demand. Yet other countries may also have raised their levels to government consumption and thus their levels of demand. Given the supply of output in the world, the area that has the largest increase in demand will find more goods flowing in and its trade balance worsening. The proper variable to explain changes in the domestic ratio of the trade balance to income is therefore not changes in the government consumption ratio, but changes in the domestic ratio relative to a weighted average in the rest of the world. A similar argument can be made for the money variable. Changes in the domestic ratio of money to income relative to the ratio in the rest of the world should be examined. The domestic value alone is insufficient.

THE GROWTH RATE VARIABLE

One additional variable other than the policy variables is included in both the trade balance and balance of payments equations. This is the growth rate variable. Mundell (1968) showed that given the rate of credit creation the growth rate should have a positive effect on the balance of payments. The faster a country grows, the more its demand for money increases. With a constant money supply, the additional money demand must be satisfied from abroad. The rate of importation of money will increase.

Laffer (1969) extended this analysis to show that increases in the growth rate of one country relative to the rest of the world is the criteria for an improved balance of payments. Given the world money supply, money will flow from where demand is relatively decreasing to where it is relatively increasing. Changes in the ratio of the balance of payments to income is therefore related to changes in the difference between the domestic growth rate and the average growth rate in the rest of the world.

The Laffer formulation is used in the balance of payments equations.

The analysis of the effect of growth rates on the trade balance is somewhat less clear. One might associate increased growth rates with increased rates of output. In such a case a positive relationship between changes in growth rate differentials and changes in the trade balance is expected. An increased relative growth rate means a larger increase in output relative to expenditure, and thus a trade balance improvement. However, recent empirical studies (Laffer and Ranson, 1973, Miles, 1974a, Laffer, 1969) have found a strong negative relationship between changes in growth rate differentials and changes in the trade balance in the major industrial countries. In his "Anti-Traditional Theory" Laffer (1969) predicted this negative relationship using a permanent income argument. In a more recent paper (1975c) he associates the growth rate with changes in expenditure. He then shows how increases in the relative rate of domestic expenditure cause the domestic relative price of nontradables to rise. The resulting substitution effects of demand and supply, as well as the income effects, are then shown to cause a deterioration in the trade balance. These arguments are outlined in more detail in Appendix A.

TESTING THE TRADE BALANCE AND BALANCE OF PAYMENTS EQUATIONS

Summarizing the discussion of this chapter, the final form of the trade balance equation is

$$\Delta(TB/Y)_i = a_0 + a_1\Delta(g_i - g_R) + a_2\Delta(M_1 - M_R) + a_3\Delta(G_i - G_R) , \qquad (4.2)$$

where

TB_i = level of the trade balance in country i

Y_i = level of output in country i

g_i, g_R = growth rates in country i and rest-of-world R

M_i, M_R = ratio of average level of high-powered money to output in country i and rest-of-world R

G_i, G_R = ratio of government consumption to output.

The balance of payments equation is

$$(BP/Y_i) = b_o + b_1\Delta(g_i - g_R) + b_2\Delta(M_i - M_R), \qquad (4.3)$$

where

BP_i = balance of payments (change in international reserves not due to allocation of SDR's)

Y_i = same as above

g_i, g_R = same as above

M_i, M_R = same as above.

The coefficients a_1, a_3, and b_2 should have negative signs. The coefficient b_1 should be positive. The sign of a_2 is indeterminant. If money is net wealth it should be negative and significant. If money is not net wealth, there is no a priori reason for either sign. The coefficient should just be statistically insignificant.

In order to prove the validity of the functional forms, equation (4.2) and (4.3) are tested for thirteen countries not in the devaluation sample. These thirteen countries consist of the U.S., Japan, eight Western European countries, plus Australia, South Africa and Mexico. The data are annual observations from the IFS tapes of the International Monetary Fund.

The trade balance is measured as the difference between f.o.b. exports and c.i.f. imports in domestic currency. The balance of payments is the change in international reserves minus the yearly allocation of SDR's. The growth rate is the difference in the natural logs of nominal income in domestic currency. The money variable is the level of currency held by the public plus the level of bank reserves at the beginning of the year, plus one-half the change in these variables minus the balance of payments.

The rest-of-world variables are constructed using a nominal GNP-weighted average of various countries. The countries used in the sample are the U.S., the U.K., Austria, Denmark, France, Germany, Italy, the Netherlands, Sweden, Switzerland, Canada, Japan, Finland and Spain. Not every country is included in each rest-of-world variable due to data limitations in some countries. For example, the growth rate variable for the rest-of-world is a weight weighted average of the growth rates of all countries above except Spain and Sweden. The monetary variable excludes Italy and Switzerland.

The results for the thirteen countries can be found in Table 2. In the absence of first-order serial correlation, the results of an ordinary least squares (OLSQ) equation are reported. Otherwise a Cochrane-Orcutt iterative technique (CORC) is used in estimating the equation. The type equation reported is indicated for each country in Table 2.

Examining the trade balance equations first, in twelve of the thirteen countries the coefficient of the growth rate differential has a negative sign. In only eight countries does the monetary policy variable have a negative sign. Government consumption has a negative coefficient in eight countries. However, not only the sign, but also the significance of the coefficients is important. The growth rate variable has a negative sign and is significant at the 95 percent level (one-tailed test) in six countries. The monetary and government consumption variables are each negative and significant in only two countries.

The results of the trade balance equation estimations are consistent with changes in the growth rate differential having a significant, negative effect on the trade balance. In all but one country the coefficient is negative, and it is significant in almost one-half the countries. The

TABLE 2

Trade Balance:
Non-Devaluation Sample

Country	Years	Equation Type	a_o	a_1	a_2	a_3	D.W.	R^2	F Statistic
U.S.	1955-73	OLSQ	-0.00	-0.20	0.08	-0.21	2.00	0.60	7.40
			(1.09)	(4.21)	(0.67)	(2.05)			(99)
Germany	1955-73	OLSQ	0.00	-0.09	-0.19	-0.51	1.66	0.47	4.39
			(1.09)	(2.40)	(1.41)	(2.56)			
Japan	1955-73	OLSQ	0.00	-0.13	-0.37	0.55	2.10	0.68	10.7
			(1.61)	(1.80)	(1.24)	(1.33)			(99.9)
Italy	1955-73	CORC	-0.00	-0.48	0.44	-0.30	2.00	0.67	8.74
			(1.32)	(4.62)	(2.69)	(0.95)			(99.5)
Netherlands	1955-73	CORC	-0.05	-0.10	-0.02	-0.38	1.57	0.40	3.17
			(3.43)	(0.77)	(0.06)	(0.53)			(90)
Belgium	1955-73	CORC	0.01	0.56	0.69	0.55	1.77	0.39	2.80
			(2.18)	(2.74)	(1.69)	(1.04)			(90)
Austria	1955-73	CORC	-0.00	-0.15	-0.09	0.14	1.78	0.31	2.06
			(0.96)	(1.79)	(0.35)	(1.14)			
Norway	1955-73	CORC	0.00	-0.21	0.41	-0.34	2.03	0.19	1.07
			(0.99)	(1.35)	(0.51)	(0.53)			
Sweden	1955-72	CORC	0.00	-0.05	-0.06	-0.02	2.04	0.13	0.62
			(1.52)	(0.76)	(0.18)	(0.09)			
Switzerland	1958-73	OLSQ	0.00	-0.23	0.03	0.34	1.55	0.15	0.75
			(0.10)	(1.31)	(0.10)	(0.54)			
Australia	1955-73	CORC	0.00	-0.03	-0.34	-0.51	1.91	0.31	2.05
			(0.84)	(0.20)	(1.06)	(0.55)			
South Africa	1955-73	OLSQ	0.00	-0.15	-0.96	-0.99	2.34	0.52	5.41
			(0.37)	(0.86)	(2.74)	(1.62)			(99)
Mexico	1955-68	CORC	-0.00	-0.15	-0.72	-0.10	2.48	0.58	4.12
			(0.03)	(3.17)	(2.10)	(0.31)			(95)

D.W. is the Durbin-Watson Statistic
Numbers in parentheses below coefficients are t-statistics
Numbers in parentheses below F-statistics are significance levels

results are not consistent, however, with the money supply having a strong, negative effect. The monetary variable is statistically significant in only two of the thirteen countries. In addition the two countries where the coefficient is significant, South Africa and Mexico, are precisely the two countries where one would expect additions to the money supply to have such an effect. Increases in the money supply should have an effect on the trade balance only if net wealth is created, i.e., if no liability is simultaneously issued with the money asset. The only situation in which this condition is guaranteed is where increases in the money supply are caused by increases in metallic money. Selling mined gold or silver to the central bank in exchange for paper currency increases bank reserves without creating an offsetting liability. It is not surprising therefore to find that the money supply has a significant effect on the trade balance in South Africa, the world's leading supplier of gold, and in Mexico, the world's leading supplier of silver. In none of the remaining countries, which all rely on fiat money for their currency, does money have a significant negative effect. The results are consistent with fiat money not being net wealth. The results are also not consistent with government consumption having a strong negative effect on the trade balance, perhaps indicating a rapid crowding out effect.

The results of the balance of payments equations in Table 3 are even more striking. The coefficient of the growth rate differential has the predicted positive coefficient in eight of the thirteen countries. It is positive and significant in only two countries. On the other hand, the monetary policy variable has a negative coefficient in ten of the thirteen countries. The coefficient is negative and significant in eight of the countries. Monetary policy clearly has an important effect on the

TABLE 3

Balance of Payments:
Non-Devaluation Sample

Country	Years	Equation Type	b_o	b_1	b_2	D.W.	R^2	F Statistic
U.S.	1955-73	CORC	-0.00	-0.02	-0.22	2.08	0.42	5.34
			(0.47)	(0.34)	(2.87)			(97.5)
Germany	1955-73	OLSQ	0.00	0.20	-1.03	2.13	0.68	16.8
			(0.98)	(2.79)	(3.78)			(99.9)
Japan	1955-73	OLSQ	0.00	-0.02	-1.13	2.15	0.59	11.5
			(1.50)	(0.32)	(3.49)			(99.9)
Italy	1955-73	CORC	-0.00	-0.12	0.33	2.56	0.29	2.83
			(1.28)	(1.25)	(1.91)			(90)
Netherlands	1955-73	CORC	-0.00	0.03	-1.70	1.95	0.71	18.5
			(1.42)	(0.28)	(4.51)			(99.9)
Belgium	1955-73	CORC	-0.00	0.05	-1.25	2.13	0.73	19.3
			(1.54)	(0.25)	(3.01)			(99.9)
Austria	1955-73	OLSQ	-0.00	0.07	0.42	1.89	0.08	0.72
			(0.26)	(0.60)	(1.13)			
Norway	1955-73	CORC	-0.00	0.03	-0.40	2.09	0.31	3.37
			(0.35)	(0.53)	(1.32)			(90)
Sweden	1955-72	CORC	0.00	0.08	-0.26	2.01	0.44	5.52
			(0.51)	(1.65)	(1.03)			
Switzerland	1958-73	CORC	0.00	0.60	0.07	2.83	0.54	7.14
			(0.00)	(3.75)	(0.25)			(99)
Australia	1955-73	CORC	-0.00	0.04	-1.07	2.10	0.55	9.29
			(0.08)	(0.25)	(3.60)			(99.5)
South Africa	1955-73	CORC	0.00	-0.26	-1.55	2.01	0.94	118.4
			(0.97)	(2.41)	(11.3)			(99.9)
Mexico	1955-68	CORC	-0.00	-0.05	-1.39	1.79	0.54	5.97
			(0.19)	(0.99)	(2.70)			(97.5)

D.W. is the Durbin-Watson Statistic
Numbers in parentheses below coefficients are t-statistics
Numbers in parentheses below F statistics are significance levels

balance of payments. Increasing the domestic portion of high-powered money clearly causes the balance of payments to deteriorate. The money supply effect dominates the growth rate effect in almost every country. In addition, in one of the two countries where the growth rate variable is significant, Germany, the effect is not unexpected. The Bundesbank is limited in its powers to create money, so one would expect Germany to rely heavily on the balance of payments to satisfy the growing demand for money. A strong positive relationship between changes in the balance of payments and changes in the growth rate differential is therefore indicated.

The empirical results of this sample provide a strong verification of the functional forms used in the ensuing tests. The coefficients of the equation have tended to have the correct sign and to generally conform to our expectations. Given the results of this sample, the functional forms can now be used to standardize for policy and growth variables in the devaluing countries. It can then be determined if devaluation alone has a significant effect on the trade balance and/or the balance of payments.

Chapter V

THE EFFECTS OF DEVALUATION ON THE TRADE BALANCE

In this chapter the techniques used to estimate the effects of government policies and growth in Chapter IV are applied to the trade balance equations of the devaluing countries. There are eighteen countries in the devaluation sample, involving twenty-six devaluations. Additional devaluations occurred in the post-war period, but data limitations reduced the analysis to these eighteen countries. The results of using equation (4.2) on this sample are shown in Table 4.

In the eighteen trade balance equations, the coefficient on changes in the growth rate differential is negative in seven cases. The coefficients on changes in the monetary and government consumption policy variables are negative in ten and twelve cases respectively. The two policy variables have negative signs in about the same percentage of countries as in the non-devaluation sample. The growth rate variable has negative coefficients in a smaller percentage of countries than in the other sample. There are four countries with growth rate coefficients that are negative and significant at the 95 percent level (one-tailed test). In three countries the government consumption policy is negative and significant, and in two countries for the monetary policy.

TABLE 4

TRADE BALANCE:
DEVALUATION SAMPLE

Country	Years	Equation Type	Devaluation Year	a_0	a_1
United Kingdom	1955-73	OLSQ	1967	-0.00	0.10
				(0.08)	(0.87)
Denmark	1955-73	CORC	1967	-0.00	-0.26
				(0.15)	(1.62)
France	1955-73	OLSQ	1957-58	-0.00	-0.16
			1969	(0.63)	(3.37)
Finland	1955-73	CORC	1957	-0.00	0.07
			1967	(0.52)	(0.38)
Iceland	1955-72	CORC	1960-61	0.00	0.43
			1967-68	(0.01)	(3.22)
Ireland	1955-73	OLSQ	1967	0.00	0.27
				(0.20)	(0.91)
Spain	1955-72	OLSQ	1957-58-59	-0.00	-0.15
			1967	(0.59)	(2.05)
New Zealand	1955-72	CORC	1967	0.00	0.11
				(0.86)	(0.58)
Costa Rica	1955-72	CORC	1961	0.00	-0.32
				(0.57)	(1.59)
Ecuador	1955-72	CORC	1961	-0.00	-0.16
			1970	(0.75)	(1.11)
Peru	1955-70	OLSQ	1958-59	0.01	0.28
			1967	(1.03)	(1.89)
Guyana	1957-73	CORC	1967	-0.00	-0.59
				(0.14)	(3.95)
Israel	1955-72	CORC	1962	0.01	-0.50
			1967	(1.24)	(3.37)
Sri Lanka	1955-72	CORC	1967	-0.00	0.14
				(0.13)	(0.77)
Philippines	1955-72	CORC	1962	0.00	0.10
			1970	(0.49)	(1.23)
Mauritius	1961-72	OLSQ	1967	0.01	0.11
				(0.76)	(0.82)
Tunisia	1962-73	OLSQ	1964	0.00	0.10
				(0.37)	(1.03)
Ghana	1957-72	CORC	1967	0.00	0.02
				(0.51)	(0.13)

D.W. is the Durbin-Watson Statistic
Numbers in parentheses below coefficients are t-statistics
Numbers in parentheses below F-statistic are significance levels.

a_2	a_3	D.W.	R^2	F Statistic
-0.04 (0.55)	0.60 (1.31)	1.98	0.20	1.23
0.33 (1.08)	0.12 (0.37)	2.18	0.37	2.73 (90.0)
-0.22 (1.58)	-0.18 (0.74)	1.79	0.46	4.34 (97.5)
-0.18 (0.31)	0.02 (0.03)	1.83	0.03	0.17
-0.19 (0.54)	-0.96 (0.73)	2.27	0.40	2.94 (90.0)
0.00 (0.02)	-0.28 (0.34)	1.88	0.11	0.64
0.06 (0.14)	-0.05 (0.26)	2.01	0.23	1.41
0.39 (0.86)	-0.65 (0.59)	2.37	0.24	1.39
-0.57 (0.87)	-2.26 (2.52)	2.02	0.47	3.82 (95.0)
-1.10 (2.50)	-0.46 (0.86)	1.73	0.47	3.85 (95.0)
-0.33 (0.55)	-0.23 (0.27)	1.67	0.23	1.20
0.51 (0.64)	0.53 (0.66)	1.63	0.58	5.54 (97.5)
-0.22 (0.52)	-0.77 (3.46)	1.78	0.41	3.01 (90.0)
-0.98 (2.21)	0.95 (1.05)	1.89	0.43	3.30 (90.0)
0.08 (0.23)	1.94 (2.55)	1.95	0.39	2.82 (90.0)
-0.13 (0.16)	-3.68 (2.25)	1.59	0.71	6.48 (97.5)
0.57 (1.42)	-0.59 (0.70)	2.05	0.34	1.40
0.07 (0.33)	-0.70 (0.93)	1.64	0.38	2.26

TESTING THE EXCHANGE RATE DIRECTLY

One method of testing the effects of devaluation is to include an exchange rate variable in equation (4.2). The statistical significance of the exchange rate coefficient then gives one indication of the importance of the exchange rate variable in affecting the trade balance. This test is performed for three different definitions of the exchange rate. Definition One is just the end of year value in units of domestic currency per dollar. Definition Two is a comparison of the domestic exchange rate to a weighted average of exchange rates in the rest of the world. There are two types of devaluation. One is to devalue relative to the U.S. dollar. The other is to devalue relative to other currencies. Definition Two should reflect both types of devaluations. Again nominal GNP is used to weight the rest-of-world variables. Definition Three is simply a dummy variable which takes the value one in years of devaluation, but zero in all other years.

In order to be consistent with equation (4.2) changes in the exchange rate rather than exchange rate levels are used. Equation (4.2) becomes

$$\Delta(TB/Y)_i = a_o\Delta(g_i - g_R) + a_2\Delta(M_i - M_R) + a_3\Delta(G_i - G_R) + a_4\Delta ER_i \ , \qquad (5.1)$$

where ER_i equals the first difference of the exchange rate in country i. The results of this test can be seen in Table 5.

Only one of the three equations for each country are reported in Table 5. In most countries it makes little difference which definition of the exchange rate is used. The equations reported are generally the ones using Definition Two. This definition is most consistent with the other variables in the equation which compare domestic to rest-of-world values. The two exceptions are Spain and Ghana. The choice of exchange rate variable significantly affects the equation in these countries. The Spain equation uses the reported exchange rate and the Ghana equation uses a dummy variable.

Since the exchange rate variable is measured in Definition Two as units of domestic currency per unit of foreign currency, a significant effect in improving the trade balance would be indicated by a positive, significant coefficient. Using this criteria the exchange rate is significant at the 95 percent level in only two of the eighteen countries, Ghana and France.

EXAMINING THE RESIDUALS

An alternative test of the effects of devaluation is to examine the behavior of the equation residuals following devaluation. This test is similar to one employed by Fama, Fisher, Jensen and Roll (1969). The coefficients of the policy and growth variables provide a method of standardizing for the effects of those variables. Using the estimated coefficients and actual values of changes in the growth rate differential, the money ratio differential and the government consumption ratio differential, fitted values for changes in the trade balance are obtained. Subtracting the fitted values from the actual values yields the residuals of the equation. The residuals represent changes in the trade balance that are due to all other variables including devaluation.

Examination of these residuals around the period of devaluation provides information about the effectiveness of devaluation. For example, if devaluation causes a permanent improvement in the trade balance, there should be large positive residuals at or near the year of devaluation and only small or random residuals in subsequent years. The large positive residuals indicate a large positive change in the trade balance that is not explained by government monetary or consumption policy or by growth

TABLE 5

Trade Balance:
Devaluation Sample Including Exchange Rates

Country	Years	Equation Type	Devaluation Year	a_o	a_1
United Kingdom	1955-73	CORC	1967	-0.00 (0.85)	-0.18 (1.54)
Denmark	1955-73	CORC	1967	-0.00 (0.20)	-0.27 (1.57)
France	1955-73	CORC	1957-58 1969	-0.00 (1.20)	-0.29 (5.30)
Finland	1955-73	CORC	1957 1967	-0.00 (0.56)	0.04 (0.24)
Iceland	1955-72	CORC	1960-61 1967-68	-0.00 (0.53)	0.39 (2.86)
Ireland	1955-73	OLSQ	1967	0.00 (0.35)	0.25 (0.82)
Spain	1955-72	OLSQ	1957-58-59 1967	-0.00 (0.32)	-0.16 (2.02)
New Zealand	1955-72	CORC	1967	0.01 (1.26)	0.14 (0.78)
Costa Rica	1955-72	CORC	1961	0.00 (0.59)	-0.29 (1.33)
Ecuador	1955-72	CORC	1961 1970	0.00 (0.71)	-0.15 (0.85)
Peru	1955-70	OLSQ	1958-59 1967	0.01 (0.87)	0.27 (1.72)
Guyana	1955-73	CORC	1967	-0.00 (0.13)	-0.57 (3.43)
Israel	1955-72	CORC	1962 1967	0.01 (1.08)	-0.52 (3.26)
Sri Lanka	1955-72	CORC	1967	-0.00 (0.13)	0.14 (0.75)
Philippines	1955-72	CORC	1962 1970	0.00 (0.33)	0.09 (1.01)
Mauritius	1961-72	OLSQ	1967	0.01 (0.73)	0.10 (0.85)
Tunisia	1962-73	CORC	1964	0.00 (0.11)	0.16 (1.59)
Ghana	1957-72	CORC	1967	-0.00 (0.48)	0.16 (1.10)

D.W. is the Durbin-Watson Statistic.
Numbers in parentheses below coefficients are t-statistics.
Numbers in parentheses below F-statistic are significance levels.

a_2	a_3	a_4	D.W.	R^2	F Statistic
-0.10	0.45	-54.0	1.58	0.55	3.91
(1.81)	(1.33)	(3.80)			(95.0)
0.33	0.14	-0.42	2.18	0.37	1.91
(1.05)	(0.38)	(0.14)			
-0.11	-0.52	2.77	1.72	0.67	6.52
(0.84)	(2.57)	(3.56)			(99.5)
-0.29	-0.20	1.96	1.93	0.10	0.37
(0.48)	(0.26)	(1.01)			
0.14	-1.37	-0.12	2.30	0.44	2.38
(0.37)	(0.99)	(0.92)			(90.0)
0.00	-0.31	34.05	1.93	0.14	0.55
(0.06)	(0.36)	(0.59)			
-0.00	-0.06	-0.00	1.99	0.24	1.05
(0.02)	(0.27)	(0.44)			
0.42	-0.55	36.72	2.39	0.34	1.51
(0.95)	(0.52)	(1.29)			
-0.49	-2.41	1.03	1.98	0.47	2.67
(0.68)	(2.26)	(0.27)			
-1.09	-0.42	-0.07	1.71	0.47	2.67
(2.35)	(0.65)	(0.12)			
-0.29	-0.15	0.09	1.71	0.24	0.85
(0.45)	(0.17)	(0.24)			
0.62	0.44	-12.4	1.69	0.59	3.94
(0.69)	(0.52)	(0.51)			(95.0)
-0.28	-0.78	1.06	1.85	0.42	2.13
(0.62)	(3.40)	(0.37)			(90.0)
-0.97	0.96	0.40	1.87	0.43	2.29
(2.06)	(1.01)	(0.11)			
0.08	1.84	0.17	1.94	0.40	1.96
(0.21)	(1.95)	(0.17)			
0.07	-3.64	-12.9	1.87	0.78	6.14
(0.09)	(2.39)	(1.48)			
0.97	-0.55	-29.7	1.90	0.58	2.03
(1.84)	(0.80)	(1.20)			
-0.22	-0.77	0.09	1.43	0.59	3.56
(1.03)	(1.20)	(2.41)			

rates. The subsequent small residuals would indicate little change in the trade balance in the future that was not due to the two policies or growth rates.

The Monetary Approach suggests that there should be only a temporary improvement in the trade balance. A temporary improvement would be indicated by positive residuals at or near the year of devaluation and negative residuals in subsequent years. This pattern of residuals would indicate a positive change in the trade balance not explained by the standardized variables, followed by eventual negative changes as the trade balance returns to its original level. If the trade balance is to return to its original level, the sum of the positive residuals should approximate the sum of the negative residuals.

A third possible path of behavior is the so-called J-curve. Under this hypothesis, devaluation causes the trade balance to worsen initially, due to price effects, but eventually to improve as demand for the country's goods increases. This hypothesis would be consistent with initially large negative residuals followed by large positive residuals. If the trade balance eventually improves, the sum of the positive residuals must exceed the sum of the negative residuals.

The residuals are examined for all countries for three years before and three years after as well as the year of devaluation. If devaluation improves the trade balance, the improvement will surely occur within three years.

The twenty-six devaluations of the eighteen countries are divided into two groups. Group I is those devaluations for which observations are available for all seven years around devaluation. Group II contains devaluations which are missing one or more observations due to data limitations, or cases in which a country had devalued in two or three consecutive years. Group I contains seventeen devaluations of sixteen countries, while Group II contains nine devaluations of eight countries.

In each country the year of devaluation is called year t. Residuals are collected for that country for the seven years t-3 to t+3. The residuals of similar periods (with respect to devaluation) are then examined across countries by creating average residuals. For example, the residuals of all countries in the year of devaluation t are summed and divided by the number of countries in the group. The resulting number represents the average residual of all the countries in the year of devaluation. This procedure is repeated for the other six time periods. The average residuals can then be compared from three years before until three years after devaluation.

The results of this procedure are shown in Table 6. Examine first the results from Group I (the seventeen devaluations). The average residuals are negative two and three years before devaluation. There is a positive residual in the year before. In the year of devaluation, however, there is an extremely large negative residual. It is more than 20 percent larger in absolute size than the residual in any of the other seven years. In the following three years there is one positive residual followed by two negative residuals. The only positive residual following devaluation is in year t+1. But this positive residual is only about one-half the absolute size of the negative residuals in the year of devaluation or in year t+2. There is no evidence of devaluation improving the trade balance even temporarily. Devaluation has a very negative effect in year t and continues to have a net negative effect in the following three years. In fact the trade balance deteriorates even more following year t+1.

Examining the residuals of each devaluation individually reveals that in nine of the seventeen devaluations the residuals behave similarly to the behavior of

TABLE 6

Total and Average Residuals:
Trade Balance

Time Period		t-3	t-2	t-1	t	t+1	t+2	t+3
Sample 1	Total	-0.0630	-0.1471	+0.0682	-0.1837	+0.0814	-0.1462	-0.1045
17 Devaluations	Average	-0.0037	-0.0087	+0.0040	-0.0108	+0.0048	-0.0086	-0.0061
Sample 1	Total	+0.0447	-0.0812	+0.0404	-0.0756	+0.0919	-0.0658	-0.0736
Excluding	Average	+0.0037	-0.0062	+0.0034	-0.0063	+0.0077	-0.0055	-0.0061
"Large" Residuals								
12 Devaluations								
Sample 1 + 2	Total	-0.0619	-0.1346	+0.0444	-0.2362	+0.1273	-0.0097	-0.1523
	Average	-0.0026	-0.0054	+0.0077	-0.0091	+0.0049	-0.0004	-0.0063

t = Year of Devaluation.

the sample average, i.e., no improvement. In six cases devaluation seems to improve the trade balance. These cases include the two countries which have significantly positive exchange rate coefficients, France and Ghana, plus Finland, Spain, New Zealand and Peru. In the remaining two cases, the United Kingdom and Guyana, the initial deterioration is just about offset by improvements in the next one or two years. But although the trade balance eventually returns to its original level in the two cases, it is more negative than expected in the intervening period. In addition the eventual return to the original level is followed by strongly negative residuals in the third year following devaluation.

The average residuals are examined in two more ways to determine if the results depend on some peculiar behavior of the seventeen devaluations included in Group I. First those devaluations with particularly large variances of the residuals are removed from the sample. Simple averaging of the residuals over seventeen cases means that those cases with the largest residuals will receive the greatest weight in the average. Removing the countries with large residuals increases the weight of other countries. Therefore countries with residuals of absolute size of at least 0.0300 in three or more years are excluded. This criterion removes five countries. However, removing these cases does not greatly change the basic results of above. The average residual for the remaining twelve countries is negative in year t. The average residual in year t+1 is positive and about the same absolute magnitude as in year t. Thus the deterioration of the trade balance in year t is offset by an improvement in year t+1. However, the average residuals in year t+2 and t+3 are strongly negative. There is evidence of a short-lived J-curve, but only in the sense that the trade balance temporarily returns to its pre-devaluation level. There is no significant improvement.

The second method of comparison is to add the devaluations of Group II to those of Group I. Group II is the sample with only partial observations or multiple devaluations. The multiple devaluations are Peru 1958-59, France 1957-58, Iceland 1960-61 and 1967-68, and Spain 1957-58-59. The year t is taken to be 1958 in Peru, France and Spain, and 1960 and 1967 in Iceland. Partial observations are

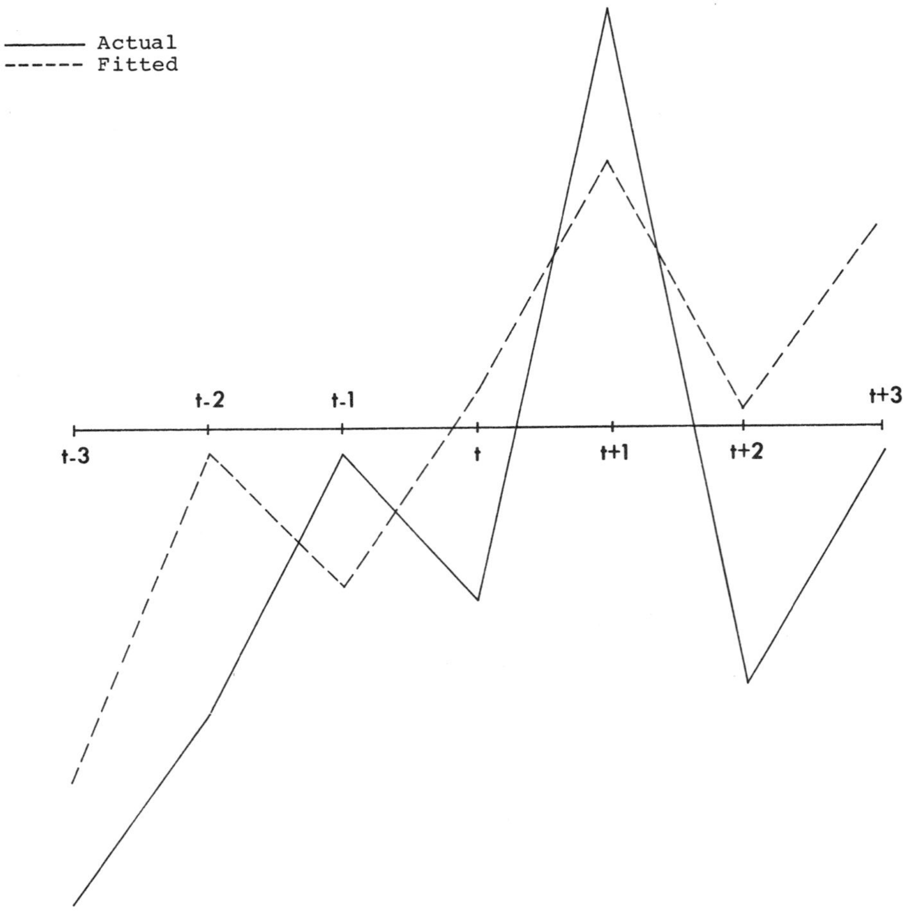

Figure 9: Change in the ratio of the trade balance to GNP (average per country).

handled by adding the residuals whenever available, and dividing the total residuals for any year by the total number of countries for which residuals are added.

The results of this test are also presented in Table 6. Adding these nine devaluations to the seventeen devaluations in the first sample still provides no evidence of even a temporary improvement in the trade balance.

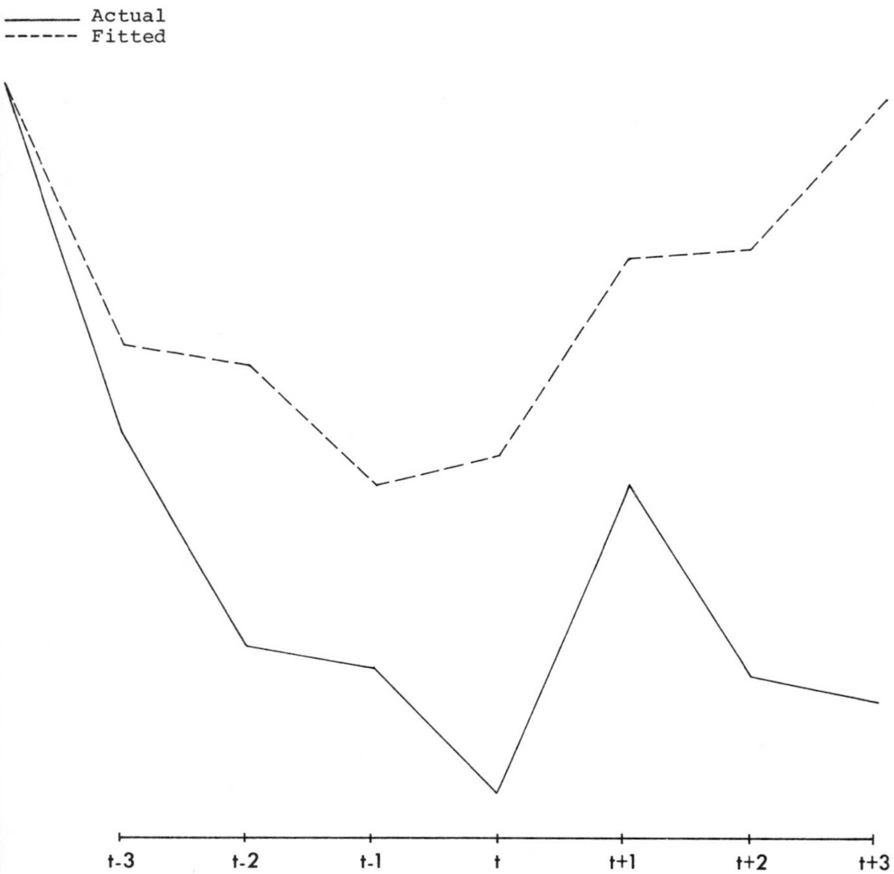

Figure 10: Ratio of the trade balance to GNP (average per country).

The pattern again is a large deterioration of the trade balance in year t followed by an improvement of about one-half that size in year t+1 and no change or deterioration in the following years.

These patterns of behavior are shown again in Figures 9 and 10. Figure 9 shows the plot of actual and fitted changes in the trade balance for the seventeen countries of Group I. Notice that the actual changes exceed the fitted changes only in the year preceding and the year following devaluation.

Figure 10 plots the cumulative sum of the actual and fitted values. Starting from a common value of TB/Y, Figure 10 is therefore equivalent to looking at actual and fitted values of TB/Y rather than Δ(TB/Y). The graph clearly shows that the actual and predicted values diverge, especially following devaluation. The actual value of TB/Y becomes increasingly smaller than the predicted value. Devaluation shortens the gap only in the year following devaluation. But even in that year the gap between actual and predicted values is larger than before devaluation.

Chapter VI

THE EFFECTS OF DEVALUATION ON THE BALANCE OF PAYMENTS

The procedures used in Chapter V for testing the effects of devaluation on the trade balance are repeated for the balance of payments. First, the balance of payments equations are estimated for each country in the devaluation sample using equation (4.3). Again there are eighteen countries encompassing twenty-six devaluations. The results of these estimations are shown in Table 7.

Recall that the growth rate differential variable is expected to have a positive coefficient and the money ratio differential to have a negative coefficient. The growth rate and monetary variables both have coefficients of the predicted sign in thirteen of the eighteen equations. Again this is approximately the same rate as in the non-devaluation sample presented in Chapter IV. The growth rate variable coefficient, however, is positive and statistically significant at the 95 percent level in only one country. On the other hand, the monetary variable has a negative coefficient that is statistically significant in eight countries. The results are consistent with monetary policy being significantly more important than growth rates in determining the balance of payments.

TABLE 7

Balance of Payments:
Devaluation Sample

Country	Years	Equation Type	Devaluation Year	b_0	b_1
United Kingdom	1955-73	CORC	1967	0.00 (0.46)	0.04 (0.34)
Denmark	1955-73	CORC	1967	0.00 (0.27)	-0.08 (0.69)
France	1955-73	OLSQ	1957-58 1969	-0.00 (0.58)	-0.04 (0.45)
Finland	1955-73	CORC	1957 1967	-0.00 (0.40)	0.61 (0.71)
Iceland	1955-72	CORC	1960-61 1967-68	0.00 (0.22)	0.24 (2.98)
Ireland	1955-73	CORC	1967	-0.00 (0.37)	0.35 (1.20)
Spain	1955-72	OLSQ	1957-58-59 1967	0.00 (0.62)	-0.11 (2.14)
New Zealand	1955-72	CORC	1967	0.00 (0.71)	0.04 (0.59)
Costa Rica	1955-72	CORC	1961	0.00 (0.21)	0.11 (0.88)
Ecuador	1955-72	CORC	1961 1970	0.00 (1.48)	0.02 (0.23)
Peru	1955-70	CORC	1958-59 1967	0.00 (0.13)	-0.00 (0.04)
Guyana	1955-73	OLSQ	1967	-0.01 (1.60)	0.06 (0.62)
Israel	1955-72	CORC	1962 1967	0.00 (0.37)	0.12 (0.65)
Sri Lanka	1955-72	CORC	1967	0.00 (0.36)	0.04 (0.69)
Philippines	1955-72	CORC	1962 1970	0.00 (1.23)	0.00 (0.02)
Mauritius	1961-72	CORC	1967	0.01 (0.91)	0.02 (0.30)
Tunisia	1962-73	CORC	1964	0.00 (1.33)	0.11 (1.24)
Ghana	1957-72	CORC	1967	0.00 (0.58)	0.09 (0.55)

D.W. is the Durbin-Watson Statistic

Numbers in parentheses below coefficients are t-statistics

Numbers in parentheses below F-statistic are significance levels.

b_2	D.W.	R^2	F Statistic
-0.11	2.57	0.68	16.03
(2.32)			(99.9)
-0.44	2.06	0.30	3.23
(1.86)			(90.0)
-0.58	1.93	0.31	3.58
(2.67)			(90.0)
-1.32	1.62	0.47	6.65
(3.62)			(99.0)
-0.05	2.19	0.39	4.42
(0.26)			(95.0)
0.20	2.42	0.31	3.42
(0.97)			(90.0)
0.06	1.91	0.26	2.41
(0.20)			(90.0)
-0.24	1.69	0.50	6.99
(1.28)			(99.0)
0.05	2.18	0.41	4.85
(0.34)			(95.0)
-0.56	2.53	0.51	7.43
(2.44)			(99.0)
0.27	2.06	0.17	1.23
(1.23)			
0.97	1.61	0.47	7.09
(3.63)			(99.0)
-0.00	1.98	0.06	0.42
(0.01)			
-0.70	2.13	0.60	10.34
(4.16)			(99.5)
-0.25	2.14	0.46	6.00
(1.37)			(97.5)
-1.09	2.14	0.47	3.57
(2.58)			(90.0)
-0.08	2.08	0.56	5.00
(0.16)			(95.0)
-0.45	2.20	0.38	3.67
(2.28)			

A DIRECT TEST OF THE EXCHANGE RATE

The first test of the effect of devaluation is to include changes in the exchange rate directly into equation (4.3). Equation (4.3) becomes

$$\Delta(BP/Y)_i = b_0 + b_i\Delta(g_i - g_R) + b_2\Delta(M_i - M_R) + b_3\Delta ER_i. \quad (6.1)$$

Again three different definitions of the exchange rate are used, the usual exchange rate, the usual exchange rate compared to a weighted average of rest-of-world exchange rates, and a dummy variable that takes the value one in years of devaluation and zero in all other years. Again in most countries it makes little difference which definition of the exchange rate is used.

The results are reported in Table 8. In all countries but Ireland, Guyana and Ghana, the exchange rate variable reported is the first difference of Definition Two, the number of domestic currency units per dollar divided by an index of rest-of-world exchange rates. In Ireland the results of using the change in the number of domestic currency units per dollar are reported. In Guyana and Ghana the results are for the dummy variable definition. In these three countries the choice of exchange rate definition makes a significant difference and the best fitting equation is chosen.

The exchange rate is measured as the number of domestic currency units per unit of foreign currency. A significant, positive effect of devaluation on the balance of payments will therefore be indicated by a significant, positive coefficient on changes in the exchange rate. This condition is fulfilled in only two of the eighteen countries, Israel and the Philippines.

RESIDUALS TEST

Just as in the trade balance analysis, an alternative test of the effect of devaluation is to examine the behavior of the equation residuals following devaluation. Using the estimated coefficients and actual values of the monetary policy and growth variables, fitted values of changes in the ratio of the balance of payments to income are obtained. These fitted values represent estimates of the changes in the balance of payments ratio that are due to the two variables. Subtracting the fitted values from the actual changes yields the equation residuals. These residuals therefore represent changes in the ratio of the balance of payments to income that are not due to growth or monetary policy. In other words the residuals represent changes that are due to all other factors including devaluation. If devaluation has a significant effect on the balance of payments, the effect should appear in the residuals.

The residuals around the period of devaluation are examined in order to look for evidence of at least a temporary improvement. As described previously, if money is net wealth, devaluation causes a reduction in real balances below their desired levels. Besides from government credit creation, the only way for the public to increase its real balances in an integrated world is through the importation of money. Devaluation therefore causes a temporary improvement in the balance of payments until real balances have been returned to their desired levels.

Even if money is not net wealth, a temporary improvement in the balance of payments is expected. For every nominal money asset the government has issued there is a bond liability. Devaluation changes the real value of both nominal assets. The real value of money assets is reduced, while the real value of bond assets is increased since real liabilities are reduced. The ratio of real money to bonds falls. Returning the ratio to its equilibrium level requires importing money and exporting bonds. The capital account and balance of payments should improve.

Since both theories predict a temporary improvement in the balance of payments, positive residuals at or near

TABLE 8

Balance of Payments:
Devaluation Sample Including Exchange Rates

Country	Years	Equation Type	Devaluation Year	b_0	b_1
United Kingdom	1955-73	CORC	1967	0.00 (0.00)	-0.01 (1.22)
Denmark	1955-73	CORC	1967	-0.00 (0.60)	-0.09 (0.79)
France	1955-73	OLSQ	1957-58 1969	-0.00 (0.50)	-0.08 (0.92)
Finland	1955-73	CORC	1957 1967	-0.00 (0.66)	0.06 (0.73)
Iceland	1955-72	CORC	1960-61 1967-68	-0.00 (0.73)	0.31 (4.11)
Ireland	1955-73	CORC	1967	0.00 (0.19)	0.56 (1.92)
Spain	1955-72	CORC	1957-58-59 1967	0.00 (0.60)	-0.11 (1.85)
New Zealand	1955-72	CORC	1967	0.00 (1.00)	0.06 (0.76)
Costa Rica	1955-72	CORC	1961	0.00 (0.26)	0.13 (0.88)
Ecuador	1955-72	CORC	1961 1970	0.00 (1.40)	0.01 (0.12)
Peru	1955-70	CORC	1958-59 1967	-0.00 (0.12)	-0.02 (0.24)
Guyana	1955-73	CORC	1967	-0.01 (1.90)	0.05 (0.47)
Israel	1955-72	CORC	1962 1967	-0.00 (0.19)	0.09 (0.55)
Sri Lanka	1955-72	CORC	1967	0.00 (0.35)	0.04 (0.69)
Philippines	1955-72	CORC	1962 1970	0.00 (0.29)	-0.00 (0.27)
Mauritius	1961-72	CORC	1967	0.01 (0.84)	0.01 (0.23)
Tunisia	1962-73	CORC	1964	0.00 (1.17)	0.11 (1.30)
Ghana	1957-72	CORC	1967	-0.00 (0.07)	0.19 (1.13)

D.W. is the Durbin-Watson Statistic.

Numbers in parentheses below coefficients are t-statistics.

Numbers in parentheses below F-statistic are significance levels.

b_2	b_3	D.W.	R^2	F Statistic
-0.12	-27.20	2.76	0.76	15.00
(2.81)	(2.21)			(99.9)
-0.42	-2.13	2.06	0.35	2.54
(1.79)	(1.05)			(90.0)
-0.47	1.94	2.06	0.38	3.09
(2.05)	(1.33)			(90.0)
-1.18	1.73	1.82	0.54	5.64
(3.30)	(1.54)			(99.0)
0.07	0.12	2.29	0.47	3.80
(0.36)	(1.69)			(95.0)
0.20	-0.88	2.24	0.49	4.50
(1.10)	(2.27)			(97.5)
0.04	-0.01	1.89	0.26	1.49
(0.13)	(0.10)			
-0.23	10.90	1.61	0.53	4.91
(1.24)	(0.94)			(97.5)
0.04	0.47	2.18	0.41	3.03
(0.20)	(0.24)			(90.0)
-0.57	-0.06	2.59	0.52	4.64
(2.37)	(0.25)			(97.5)
0.31	0.13	2.03	0.22	1.06
(1.36)	(0.87)			
1.46	0.05	1.75	0.42	3.39
(3.13)	(1.48)			(95.0)
-0.38	7.79	1.93	0.40	2.92
(0.85)	(2.76)			(90.0)
-0.69	0.39	2.11	0.60	6.46
(3.84)	(0.27)			(99.0)
-0.16	0.93	1.82	0.67	8.67
(1.11)	(2.88)			(99.5)
-1.14	3.19	2.09	0.49	2.26
(2.53)	(0.54)			
-0.14	-23.00	2.04	0.62	3.82
(0.30)	(1.16)			(90.0)
-0.67	0.07	2.01	0.49	3.51
(2.90)	(1.55)			

the year of devaluation are expected, followed by negative residuals as the balance of payments returns to its original level. The actual pattern of the residuals can be seen in Table 9. Again the residuals are examined three years before and after, as well as in the year of devaluation. Average residuals are again computed by summing the residuals across countries for similar years (with respect to devaluation). Likewise the twenty-six devaluations are divided into the same Group I and Group II as for the trade balance. Group I contains seventeen devaluations, while Group II (partial observations and multiple devaluations) contains nine devaluations.

The pattern of residuals is quite different for the balance of payments than for the trade balance. Examining the residuals in Group I finds that in the three years preceding devaluation the average residuals are negative, especially in t-1, the year before devaluation. In the year of devaluation the average residuals are strongly positive. In years t+1 and t+3 the residuals are slightly positive, but not very different from zero. In year t+2 the average residuals are negative. But since none of the improvement in the balance of payments is offset for at least two years, devaluation has clearly improved the balance of payments.

Examining the countries of Group I individually reveals that nine of the seventeen cases have positive residuals in the year of devaluation. Thirteen have positive residuals in year t+1 and nine in year t+2. Twelve of the cases have positive values in two of the three years from t to t+2. In only two countries, the United Kingdom and Ecuador, is there evidence of a continued deterioration of the balance of payments following devaluation.

Once again countries with large residuals are excluded from Group I and the average residuals are recomputed. Countries with "large" residuals are again defined as those

TABLE 9

Total and Average Residuals:
Balance of Payments

Time Period		t-3	t-2	t-1	t	t+1	t+2	t+3
Sample 1	Total	-0.0455	-0.0711	-0.1293	+0.0962	+0.0141	-0.0446	+0.0139
17 Devaluations	Average	-0.0027	-0.0042	-0.0076	+0.0057	+0.0008	-0.0026	+0.0008
Sample 1	Total	-0.0340	-0.0614	-0.1275	+0.0549	+0.0329	+0.0184	-0.0250
Excluding	Average	-0.0024	-0.0044	-0.0091	+0.0039	+0.0024	+0.0013	-0.0018
"Large" Residuals								
14 Devaluations								
Sample 1 + 2	Total	-0.0269	-0.1602	-0.1424	+0.1185	+0.0783	+0.0264	-0.0176
	Average	-0.0011	-0.0067	-0.0055	+0.0046	+0.0030	+0.0010	-0.0007

t = Year of Devaluation

with size 0.0300 or more in at least three of the seven years. Three devaluations are removed from the sample, Ireland, Guyana and Israel 1967. With these three removed, the average residuals in years t, t+1 and t+2 are all positive. The average residual in year t+3 is now negative.

Next the residuals in Group II are added to those of the entire Group I. The resulting pattern of average residuals is similar to the pattern for Group I with the large residuals removed. The average residuals are positive in years t, t+1 and t+2. The average residual in year t+3 is negative but close to zero in value. The results are still consistent with devaluation improving the balance of payments.

The fact that the average residuals are positive in three of the four years t to t+3, and that the negative

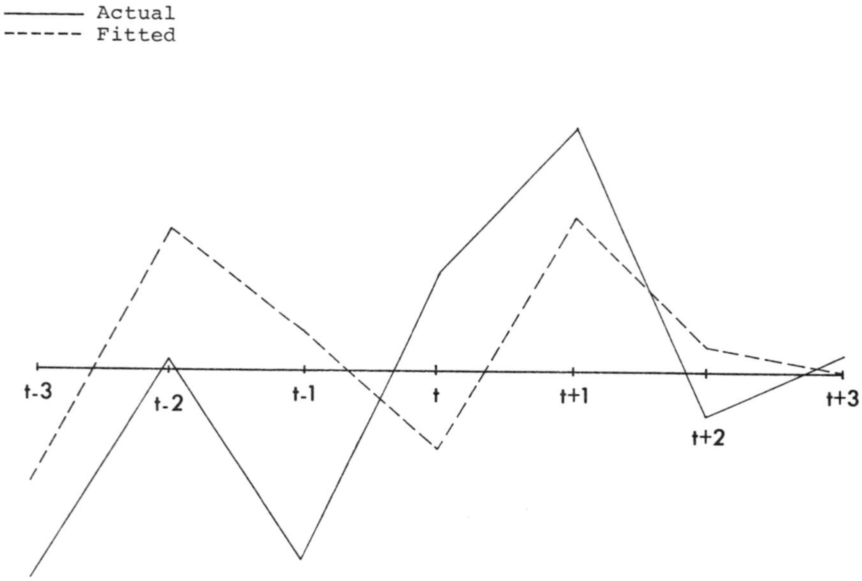

Figure 11: Changes in the ratio of the balance of payments to GNP (average per country).

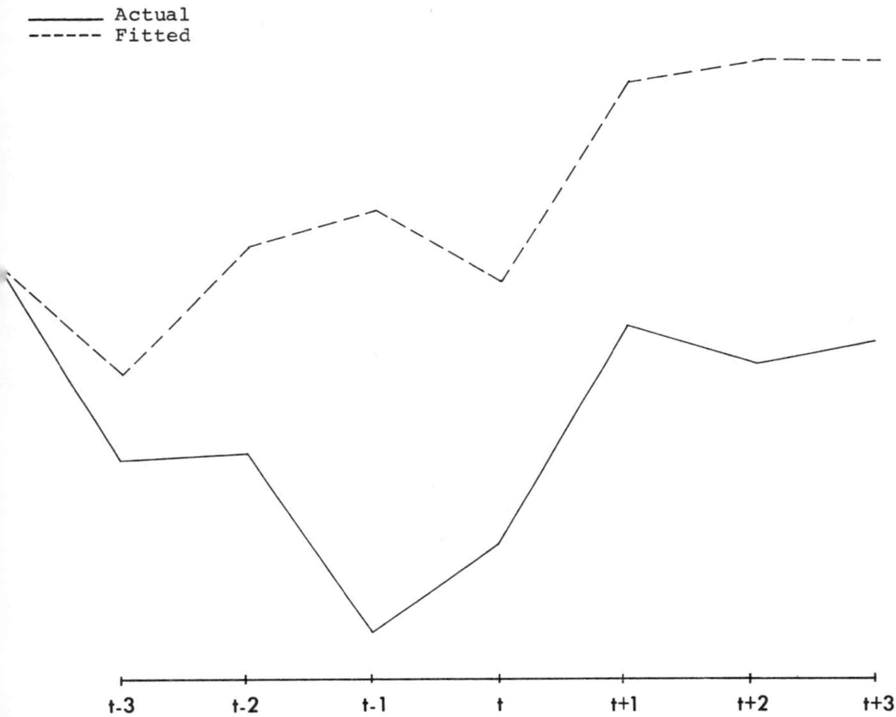

Figure 12: Ratio of the balance of payments to GNP (average per country).

residuals are not of sufficient magnitude to offset the positive ones, seems to indicate a permanent improvement in the balance of payments following devaluation. However, part of this improvement can be explained as offsetting the deterioration of the account prior to devaluation. In all three groupings of the residuals, the average residuals are negative in the three years preceding devaluation. The large deterioration may be partly due to anticipations of the devaluation. In any case the balance of payments has greatly deteriorated by the time devaluation occurs. Some of the subsequent improvement may therefore involve simply bringing the balance of payments back to a more "normal" level.

The improvement of the balance of payments following devaluation can be seen in Figures 11 and 12. Figure 11 shows actual and predicted average changes in the ratio of the balance of payments to income for the seventeen countries of Group I. Notice that the actual change exceeds the predicted change in the year of and the year following devaluation. Figure 12 shows the cumulative sum of actual and predicted values of average changes in the balance of payments ratio for Group I. Figure 12 is therefore equivalent to actual and predicted values of the ratio BP/Y. In the three years preceding devaluation, the actual and predicted values become increasingly divergent. However, in the year of devaluation and the following year this divergence is greatly reduced. The ratio of the balance of payments to income increases relative to its predicted levels following devaluation.

One final comment concerns the results of these two chapters. In Chapter V it is determined that devaluation is not consistent on average with an improvement in the trade balance. In this chapter it is determined that devaluation is consistent with an improvement in the balance of payments. If the balance of payments improves but the trade balance does not, the improvement in the balance of payments must come from the capital account. An improvement in only the capital account and balance of payments is precisely the result expected if fiat money is not viewed by the public as net wealth.

Chapter VII

FURTHER EMPIRICAL TESTS

The results of Chapters V and VI indicate that devaluation tends to improve the balance of payments, but not the trade balance. In this chapter the data are reexamined using three additional statistical techniques. The results of these tests reinforce the results of the previous chapters.

SEEMINGLY UNRELATED REGRESSIONS

The first technique is seemingly unrelated regressions (see Zellner, 1962, and Kmenta, 1971). This technique employs generalized least squares to incorporate the covariance of errors among the countries in estimating coefficients of the individual countries. One of the assumptions of ordinary least squares is that the errors of the individual country equations are unrelated. This assumption is implicit in the techniques employed in Chapters V and VI. However, it is possible that such an assumption is not valid for the trade balance and balance of payments. For the world as a whole, the sum of all trade balances or the sum of all balance of payments is constrained to be zero. For each export in the world there must be an equivalent import. Thus the trade balance and balance of payments errors for all countries in the world are not independent. The remaining questions are whether the errors of the estimated equations of the subset of countries used in the study are independent, and what effect any covariance of errors will have on the estimated coefficients.

The first step of the procedure is to estimate the individual country equations by ordinary least squares. At this stage the equations are assumed to be unrelated. However, in the second step the errors of these equations are used to create a variance-covariance matrix V. The final step is to reestimate the individual regression coefficients incorporating the information about the covariance of the errors. According to Aitken's generalized least squares formula, the estimate of the coefficient vector B is now[1]

$$B = (X'V^{-1}X)^{-1}(X'V^{-1}Y) \tag{7.1}$$

where Y is a (N (country) xT (observation) x 1) vector of the dependent variable and X is a N•T x N•K (independent variables) matrix.

Thus seemingly unrelated regressions increase the efficiency of the estimators by incorporating information about the mutual correlation of the disturbances.[2] Notice that if the errors are uncorrelated, V becomes a diagonal matrix and (7.1) reduces to

$$B = (X'X)^{-1}(X'Y) \ , \tag{7.2}$$

the formula for ordinary least squares.[3]

The sample of countries for the seemingly unrelated tests consists of fourteen of the eighteen countries used

---

[1] See Kmenta (1970, p. 520).

[2] See Kmenta (1970, p. 518).

[3] For a proof of this equivalence see Kmenta (1970, pp. 521-24).

ORDER NUMBER

PO NYAATP08

BOOK NUMBER

9820238

BAY NUMBER

4415-10

AUTHOR	Miles, M.A.
TITLE	Business Economics and Finance:

in Chapters V and VI. The tests require that all countries have observations in the same year, and the four countries eliminated have from two to seven years fewer observations than the remaining fourteen. The four countries are Peru, Mauritius, Tunisia and Ghana. Data for all remaining countries are available for the period 1955-72.

One additional problem is the possible first-order autocorrelation of the disturbances of individual countries. To handle the autocorrelation, the estimates of the autocorrelation coefficient ρ that were obtained from the iterative Cochran-Orcutt technique on the ordinary least squares are used to transform the data before the present test is performed.[4] The transformation leaves each variable in each of the fourteen countries with seventeen observations for the period 1956-1972.

The results of the seemingly unrelated regressions for the trade balance are shown in Table 10. The increased efficiency of the estimators can be seen in the increased frequency of statistically significant coefficients. The frequency of significance and signs of the trade balance coefficients both before and after the seemingly unrelated technique is summarized in Table 11. The effect of the technique on signs is very minimal. The growth rate, money and exchange rate variables all have the same frequency of positive and negative signs before and after the technique is applied.[5] Only the government consumption variable is slightly affected. There are nine negative and five positive coefficients before and ten

---

[4] See Kmenta (1970, pp. 528-29).

[5] Notice that the frequency of positive and negative monetary coefficients differs from those in Table 5. As noted, the number of observations in some countries are reduced in order to assure the same number in all countries. This reduction in observations resulted in a change of sign for Ireland's and Guyana's monetary policy coefficients.

TABLE 10

Seemingly Unrelated Regressions:
Trade Balance

Country	a_0	a_1	a_2	a_3	a_4
United Kingdom	0.00	-0.25	-0.11	-0.00	-32.3
	(0.36)	(4.63)	(4.13)	(0.01)	(3.46)
Denmark	0.00	-0.18	0.07	-0.06	0.34
	(0.23)	(1.87)	(0.39)	(0.24)	(0.16)
France	-0.00	-0.27	-0.18	-0.44	2.56
	(1.08)	(9.59)	(2.34)	(3.35)	(6.13)
Finland	-0.00	0.01	-0.25	-0.01	2.55
	(0.69)	(0.08)	(0.69)	(0.03)	(2.04)
Iceland	0.00	0.44	-0.02	-1.42	-0.10
	(0.47)	(7.07)	(0.12)	(2.13)	(1.56)
Ireland	0.01	0.15	0.06	-0.98	45.47
	(1.07)	(0.84)	(0.79)	(2.03)	(1.53)
Spain	-0.00	-0.13	-0.06	-0.04	-0.07
	(0.47)	(2.87)	(0.25)	(0.11)	(0.74)
New Zealand	0.01	0.10	0.36	0.35	36.47
	(1.10)	(1.06)	(1.79)	(0.56)	(2.35)
Costa Rica	0.00	-0.27	-0.61	-2.24	1.60
	(0.73)	(2.45)	(1.47)	(3.42)	(0.76)
Ecuador	0.00	-0.21	-1.11	-0.59	0.22
	(0.82)	(2.48)	(4.78)	(1.86)	(0.73)
Guyana	-0.00	-0.66	-0.23	0.36	-26.3
	(0.00)	(6.78)	(0.50)	(0.55)	(1.99)
Israel	0.01	-0.44	-0.26	-0.76	-0.86
	(1.43)	(4.71)	(0.87)	(5.40)	(0.46)
Sri Lanka	-0.00	0.21	-0.88	1.15	-1.77
	(0.19)	(2.87)	(4.56)	(2.80)	(0.95)
Philippines	0.00	0.13	0.09	2.03	0.28
	(0.31)	(3.51)	(0.56)	(4.69)	(0.58)

D.F. = 12
97.5% (one tail) = 2.179
95.0% " = 1.782
90.0% " = 1.356

TABLE 11

Signs and Significance of Variables Before and After Seemingly Unrelated Regressions: Trade Balance

SIGN	Before				After			
	G	M	GC	ER	G	M	GC	ER
	Signs							
+	6	4	5	8	6	4	4	8
-	8	10	9	6	8	10	10	6
	Significant (95% Level One-tailed Test)							
+	1	0	1	1	3	1	2	3
-	4	3	3	1	8	4	6	2

negative and four positive coefficients afterwards. There is now one more coefficient of the predicted sign.

However, not only the sign, but the significance of the coefficients is important. The frequency of significance at the 95 percent level (one-tailed test) of coefficients of both signs is therefore reported. For example, before the seemingly unrelated regression technique is applied, there are four negative and one positive coefficients of the growth rate variable that are significant. Applying the technique causes the rate of significance to double. There are now eight negative and three positive coefficients that are significant. Thus incorporating the covariance of the error terms leads to the growth rate variables in over half of the countries to now have significant coefficients of the predicted (negative) sign.

One may wonder why the significance of coefficients of both signs was measured. From the theory outlined in Chapters IV and Appendix A, only the number of significant negative coefficients is important. But since the seemingly unrelated regressions technique is increasing the efficiency of the estimates, it is possible that coefficients of both signs are becoming increasingly significant. It is therefore interesting to see which coefficients have a greater increase in significance. In the case of the growth rate variable, the negative coefficients clearly increase by more. The technique creates four additional significant negative coefficients but only two more positive ones.

The frequency of significant government consumption variables also doubles. There are now six negative coefficients after the technique as compared to three before. The significant positive coefficients increase from one to two. The monetary and exchange rate variables show little change. The monetary variable has one additional significant positive and one additional negative coefficient. The exchange rate variable has two additional significant positive and one additional negative coefficient.

Thus the results of applying the seemingly unrelated regression technique to the trade balance reinforce much of the previous findings. The importance of the growth rate variable is clearly reinforced. The importance of the government consumption variable is also increased. But even incorporating the covariance of the errors seems to provide little evidence of a significant effect on the trade balance of either the monetary or exchange rate variables.

The seemingly unrelated technique is similarly applied to the balance of payments equation. The results are shown in Tables 12 and 13. Again the frequency of significant coefficients is increased, and again these results reinforce the earlier findings.

The effect on the signs of the coefficient are shown in Table 13.[6] There is one more monetary coefficient and

---

[6] For the reason described in footnote 5, the frequency of positive and negative coefficients for the monetary and

TABLE 12

Seemingly Unrelated Regressions:
Balance of Payments

Country	b_0	b_1	b_2	b_3
United Kingdom	-0.00	-0.03	-0.12	-32.5
	(0.39)	(0.51)	(5.64)	(3.16)
Denmark	-0.00	-0.14	-0.58	-2.34
	(0.71)	(2.13)	(4.16)	(1.63)
France	-0.00	-0.03	-0.88	0.27
	(0.47)	(0.69)	(6.39)	(0.30)
Finland	-0.00	0.06	-1.03	1.15
	(0.23)	(1.66)	(7.52)	(2.30)
Iceland	-0.00	0.33	0.16	0.10
	(0.59)	(6.46)	(1.29)	(1.96)
Ireland	0.00	0.22	0.14	-29.7
	(0.04)	(2.38)	(2.57)	(1.34)
Spain	0.00	-0.12	-0.01	-0.07
	(0.63)	(3.79)	(0.08)	(1.01)
New Zealand	0.00	0.06	-0.22	14.53
	(1.23)	(2.16)	(3.03)	(2.26)
Costa Rica	0.00	0.18	-0.16	-0.50
	(0.25)	(2.35)	(0.69)	(0.51)
Ecuador	0.01	0.04	-0.62	-0.06
	(1.60)	(0.99)	(4.99)	(0.44)
Guyana	-0.00	-0.01	1.15	6.13
	(0.73)	(0.15)	(8.63)	(1.20)
Israel	-0.00	0.11	-0.49	6.85
	(0.01)	(1.70)	(2.96)	(6.66)
Sri Lanka	0.00	0.02	-0.69	0.36
	(0.27)	(0.36)	(7.00)	(0.43)
Philippines	0.00	-0.02	-0.25	1.04
	(0.24)	(1.53)	(3.31)	(6.11)

D.F. = 12
97.5% (one-tail) = 2.179
95.0% " = 1.782
90.0% " = 1.356

TABLE 13

Signs and Significance of Variables Before and After Seemingly Unrelated Regressions: Balance of Payments

SIGN	Variable					
	Before			After		
	G	M	ER	G	M	ER
	Signs					
+	8	4	10	8	3	8
-	6	10	4	6	11	6
	Significant (95% level one-tailed test)					
+	1	1	2	4	2	5
-	1	6	1	2	9	1

two less exchange rate coefficients of the predicted sign after the technique is applied. The frequency of signs of the growth rate coefficient is unchanged.

The changes in the frequency of significant coefficients are more marked. For example, the number of positive (predicted sign) coefficients of the growth rate variable that are significant at the 95 percent level (one-tailed test) increase from one to four.[7] The number of negative coefficients increases by only one to a total of two. The significant coefficients of the monetary variable increase from six negative (predicted sign) and one positive to nine negative and two positive. Almost two-thirds of the countries therefore have significant monetary

[6] exchange rate variables differ from Table 8. The differences are in the monetary coefficient in Costa Rica and the exchange rate coefficient in Ecuador.

[7] The difference in the frequency of initial positive growth rate and negative exchange rate coefficients from Table 8 is caused by using definition Two of the exchange rate for Ireland here, rather than definition One, as reported in Table 8.

coefficients of the predicted sign. The number of positive, significant exchange rate coefficients increases by three to a total of five, while the number of negative, significant coefficients does not change at all.

The results reinforce the previous results of a negative, significant effect of changes in domestic high-powered money on changes in the balance of payments. There is also increased evidence of a positive effect of exchange rate changes. The number of significant positive exchange rate coefficients has increased markedly relative to the number of negative ones. This result for the exchange rate is quite different than for the trade balance sample. Finally, there is increased evidence of a positive effect of changes in relative growth rates on changes in the balance of payments.

POOLED CROSS-SECTION TIME SERIES

A second technique is to constrain the coefficients of all variables to be the same in all countries. This procedure involves performing a pooled cross-section time series regression on the entire sample. The pooled cross-section time series technique is useful because, if the pooling is valid, it allows one to greatly increase the degrees of freedom of the regression equation and thus the efficiency of the estimate.

The pooled cross-section time series model used is an error components model which accounts for the existence of country specific residuals, of residuals within a country over time, as well as of autoregression. First each country's data is transformed using the estimates of ρ obtained from the iterative Cochran-Orcutt technique. Next mean values for specific countries $\bar{x}_{i.}$ and mean values over all countries $\bar{x}_{..}$ are calculated for all variables. The regression

$$\bar{y}_{i\cdot} - y_{it} = a_o + a_1 (x_{i\cdot} - x_{it}) + \ldots \qquad (7.3)$$

now allows estimates to be made of the residuals within a country over time. By subtracting individual observations of a country from the country mean, the country specific residual is eliminated. The remaining within country residual is used to estimate the variance of that residual. Similarly the regression

$$\bar{y}_{\cdot\cdot} - \bar{y}_{i\cdot} = b_o + b_1 (\bar{x}_{\cdot\cdot} - \bar{x}_{i\cdot}) + \ldots \qquad (7.4)$$

provides an estimate of the sum of the country specific and within country residuals. The estimate of the sum of the residuals is used to estimate its variance. Equations (7.3) and (7.4) are then weighted by the reciprocals of their respective estimated standard errors. The weighting is the standard method of eliminating heteroscadasticity of errors across countries. The two weighted equations are added and a regression is performed on the resulting sums.

The procedure is first used for the trade balance. At first all fourteen countries are included in the sample. However, the test for aggregation of the sample fails. The aggregation test is an F-test that asks whether constraining the coefficients to be the same in all countries significantly raises the sum of squared residuals. This test is equivalent to testing the null hypothesis that the coefficients are in fact the same across all countries. The value of the F-test for the trade balance when all countries are included is $F(52,182) = 2.98$, which can be rejected at even the 99.9 percent level. However, when the four countries with the largest residuals are eliminated, the null hypothesis can be accepted. The four countries eliminated are Iceland, Guyana, Israel and Sri Lanka. The F-test is now $F(36,130) = 1.315$, which cannot be rejected at even the 90 percent level. The estimated coefficients are:

Variable	G	M	GC	ER	
Coefficient	-0.078	-0.163	-0.318	-0.058	$\bar{R}^2=0.06$
t-statistic	(1.77)	(2.55)	(1.88)	(0.36)	

where G, M, GC and ER represent the same growth rate, monetary, government consumption and exchange rate variables referred to previously. The growth rate, monetary and government consumption variables all have the predicted negative sign and are significant at the 95 percent level (one-tailed test). The exchange rate variable, however, has the wrong sign and is not significant.

Pooling the data therefore reinforces the earlier results concerning the exchange rate. There still is no evidence of a significant positive effect of devaluation on the trade balance. Similarly the earlier indications of a significant effect of growth rates and government consumption are reinforced. However, the significant effect of the money variable differs from the earlier results.

The attempts to pool the balance of payments equations were less successful. Eliminating even six of the countries did not produce a sufficiently small F-statistic for the aggregation test. With only eight countries remaining, the F-statistic is $F(21,112) = 2.85$, a value which can be rejected at even the 99.9 percent level.

Although the aggregation test fails, the results of the pooled balance of payments equation may still be illustrative. The estimated coefficients are:

Variable	G	M	ER	
Coefficient	0.019	-0.129	0.174	$\bar{R}^2 = 0.09$
t-statistic	(0.73)	(2.68)	(2.19)	

The monetary and growth rate variables have the predicted sign as before. Also as before, the monetary variable is significant while the growth rate variable is not. However, the most interesting result is for the exchange rate. While the exchange rate coefficient of the pooled trade balance equation has the wrong sign and is not significant, the exchange rate coefficient of the balance of payments equations is positive and significant at the 95 percent level. Again there is additional evidence that devaluation does not improve the trade balance but improves the balance of payments.

INTRODUCING LEADS AND LAGS

A final procedure is to introduce lead and lag values of the exchange rate. While the contemporaneous exchange rate variable has an insignificant effect on the trade balance, it is still possible that either lagged or future values do have a significant effect. Significant lead values would indicate that traders anticipate the devaluation and adjust trade flows accordingly. Significant lagged values would be consistent with the position of J-curve proponents that it takes time for traders to fully adjust to the effects of devaluation.

The test is performed by constraining the exchange rate coefficient to be the same in all countries, but allowing all other coefficients including constants to differ. Again an F-test is used to test the null hypothesis that the exchange rate coefficient is the same in all countries. The test compares the sum of squared residuals in the constrained and unconstrained cases.

The equation with exchange rate lags and leads for the trade balance contains eight countries. Iceland, Ireland, New Zealand, Guyana, Israel and Sri Lanka have been eliminated from the sample. The F-statistic for the constraint is $F(7,128) = 0.7423$ which cannot be rejected at even the 90 percent level. The coefficients and t-statistics for the lagged, lead and contemporaneous exchange rate terms are:

Time period	-2	-1	0	+1	+2
Coefficient	-0.155	0.018	-0.141	0.372	-0.061
t-statistic	(0.43)	(0.07)	(0.73)	(1.22)	(0.25)

Notice that none of the coefficients is significant at even the 90 percent level (one-tailed test). The only coefficient that has a t-statistic above one in value is the first lagged term. The sign of that coefficient is positive, indicating an improvement in the trade balance. Such a positive improvement in the year following devaluation is consistent with the results of the residuals test. But just as the positive residuals in the year following devaluation were smaller than the negative residuals in surrounding years, the possible positive exchange rate effect here is still not sufficiently large to indicate an overall trade balance improvement. Thus even including leads and lags does not provide evidence of a positive effect of devaluation on the trade balance.

The results for the balance of payments, however, are quite different. The balance of payments equation contains ten countries. Iceland, Ireland, Guyana and Israel are excluded from the sample. The F-statistic for the constraint is $F(9,160) = 0.8251$, which cannot be rejected at even the 90 percent level. The values of the coefficients and t-statistics are:

Time period	-2	-1	0	+1	+2
Coefficient	-0.301	-0.227	0.053	0.311	-0.389
t-statistic	(1.50)	(1.37)	(0.37)	(1.62)	(2.51)

The two lead terms are both significant at the 90 percent level (one-tailed test), the first lag term is significant at about the 95 percent level, and the second lag term is significant at the 99 percent level. Only the contemporaneous term is insignificant. The negative signs of the lead terms indicate outflows of money as individuals anticipate the devaluation. The positive coefficient of the first lag term indicates an improvement in the balance of payments in the year following devaluation. The negative sign of the second lag, however, indicates that the balance of payments then moves towards its old level. In fact, if the coefficients of the contemporaneous and two lag terms are summed, they equal -0.034 which is very close to zero.

Therefore, including lag and lead exchange rate terms in the balance of payments equation provides evidence of an improvement in the account. The improvement is temporary, lasting no more than two years. The temporary improvement is precisely the type predicted in Chapter II. On the other hand, there is no evidence of devaluation producing even a temporary improvement in the trade balance. As in the case of the balance of payments, the empirical results are consistent with the theoretical predictions of Chapter II.

Chapter VIII

SUMMARY AND CONCLUSION

This study deals with the effects of several variables on the trade balance and balance of payments. In order to organize the conclusion of the study, the results for each variable will be discussed in turn.

The main goal of the study is to determine whether devaluation improves the trade balance and the balance of payments, once government policies and growth rates are taken into account. This question is explored through several statistical techniques. Testing the exchange rate directly through ordinary least squares provides no evidence of an improvement in either account. The exchange rate coefficient is positive and significant in only two of eighteen countries. Examining the residuals of the equation without the exchange rate, however, provides a different result. The residuals indicate a small improvement in the trade balance in the year following devaluation. But this improvement is small compared to the deterioration of the trade balance in the year of devaluation or succeeding years. On the other hand, there is clear evidence of the balance of payments improving following devaluation. This pattern of contrasting behavior is reinforced by the succeeding tests. While the seemingly unrelated regressions increase the number of both positive and negative significant exchange rate coefficients for the trade balance by one, the number of positive significant coefficients for the balance of payments rises relative to the number of negative ones. Pooling the data across time and countries does not create a significant exchange rate coefficient for the trade balance, but does create a significant positive coefficient for the balance of payments. Finally, constraining only the exchange rate coefficient across countries and introducing lead and lag values further reinforces the pattern. Neither the two leads, the contemporaneous term nor the two lags of the exchange rate are significant for the trade balance. The balance of payments, however, has a clear, significant pattern. The balance of payments worsens in the years preceding devaluation. The account improves in the year following devaluation. The improvement is temporary, lasting about two years. The results of this study are therefore generally consistent with the results of most of the reported studies where there was no standardization for government policy. Here, as in those studies, devaluation is found to cause a slight improvement in the trade balance in the year following devaluation. But the improvement is small in comparison to the deterioration in surrounding years and therefore does not create a net improvement in the account. In contrast, the balance of payments is found to improve at least temporarily following devaluation.

Another variable whose effect is measured is relative growth rates. The coefficients of the variable are found to generally have the predicted sign, negative for the trade balance and positive for the balance of payments. The coefficients for trade balance, however, tend to be more frequently statistically significant and of the predicted sign than those for the balance of payments. In four of the eighteen countries the growth coefficient is negative and significant in the trade balance equation. In only one of eighteen balance of payments equations is the growth rate coefficient both significant and positive. Using the seemingly unrelated regression technique raises these numbers to eight and four out of fourteen respectively. In the pooled equations the growth rate coefficient is negative and significant for the trade balance, and positive but not significant for the balance of payments. Thus there is evidence that relative growth rates are an important determinant of the behavior of the trade balance. An increase in the growth rate of the country in question relative to the growth rate in the rest of the world worsens that country's trade balance. However, the same increase in relative growth rates tends to improve the country's balance of payments.

Government consumption also tends to have a negative effect on the trade balance. Only two of the eighteen initial regressions have a negative and significant government consumption coefficient. Employing seemingly unrelated regressions raises this number to six of fourteen countries. Finally the coefficient of the pooled equation is negative and significant. These results rule out the possibility of an immediate "crowding out" effect. They are consistent, however, with the "crowding out" effect requiring three to four quarters that is found in some domestic models.

The final variable is the monetary variable. This variable is found to have a very strong negative effect on the balance of payments, but the results are mixed for the trade balance. Only three of the eighteen initial trade balance equations have negative and significant monetary variable coefficients. The seemingly unrelated regression technique raises this number to only four of fourteen. Yet the monetary variable coefficient in the pooled equation is negative and significant. The results are inconclusive for the trade balance. In contrast, in eight of the initial eighteen balance of payments equations the monetary variable coefficient is negative and significant. This number rises to nine of fourteen countries when seemingly unrelated regressions are used. In addition the coefficient in the pooled equation is negative and significant. A relative increase in the money supply by the government clearly worsens the balance of payments.

Finally, combining the results of the trade balance, the balance of payments and the money variable provides evidence that fiat money may not be considered net wealth by money holders. The lack of improvement in the trade balance following devaluation and the inconclusive effect of the money variables on the trade balance are both consistent with the absence of a real cash balance effect. However, the improvement in the balance of payments following devaluation shows that some type of monetary adjustment still takes place. What may be occurring therefore in the case of devaluation or a money supply change is a simple portfolio adjustment. Devaluation causes an adjustment in the holding of money relative to bonds, but fails to affect any real variable such as wealth, expenditure or the trade balance.

Appendix A

THEORETICAL MODELS RELATING CHANGES IN RELATIVE GROWTH RATES TO CHANGES IN THE TRADE BALANCE

The negative relationship between changes in a country's growth rate relative to the rest of the world and changes in the country's ratio of the trade balance to income has been suggested in three theoretical papers. The first paper is Laffer's "An Anti-Traditional Theory of the Balance-of-Payments Under Fixed Exchange Rates". In the paper the functional form is derived by adding a permanent income argument to a Keynesian absorption model. The trade balance portion of the model involves basically three equations, an export function, an expenditure function, and an import function. The basic export function of country i is of the form

$$X_i = b_i + x_i \cdot Y_i \tag{1}$$

where X is the level of exports, y is the level of output or income and x is the marginal propensity to export. The coefficient x is assumed positive and constant. The level of exports therefore is assumed to rise with income.

The expenditure function of country i is

$$E_i = d_i + c_i \cdot Y_i + e_i \cdot \Delta Y_i \tag{2}$$

where E is the level of expenditure, d, c, e are constants and ΔY is the change in output or income. The expenditure function is of a basic Keynesian form, except for the addition of the change in income term. The term cY represents the Keynesian assumption that expenditure rises with the level of income. But the term $e\Delta Y$ represents a quite different assumption. This term relates expenditure to wealth rather than to income. ΔY is the rate at which income is increasing. If the rate is expected to continue, the rate together with the present level of Y define a unique level of permanent income. Therefore, given the present level of Y, increases in ΔY represent increases in future income, and thus permanent income. Assuming expenditure to be a positive function of permanent income, increases in ΔY will cause E to rise.

The import function is derived by substituting (1) and (2) above into the absorption relationship

$$TB_i = X_i - M_i = Y_i - E_i \ . \qquad (3)$$

This yields

$$\begin{aligned} M_i &= X_i + E_i - Y_i \\ &= b_i + x_i \cdot Y_i + d_i + c_i \cdot Y_i + e_i \cdot \Delta Y_i - Y_i \\ &= (b_i + d_i) + (x_i + c_i - 1)\, Y_i + e_i \cdot \Delta Y_i \ . \end{aligned}$$

Again the equation has two parts. The first part is the constant term and the Keynesian relationship that imports are a positive function of income. The second part relates the demand for imports positively to permanent income, as in the expenditure equation above.

In order to get these equations in the growth differential form two additional factors have to be accounted for. One factor is the relative size of the country, and the other is the real rate of interest. The relative size relationship is handled through the export function. The export equation of country i becomes

$$X_i = b_i + x_i . Y_i + v_i . p_i \qquad (4)$$

where p_i is defined as

$$p_i = \frac{Y_i}{\Sigma Y_i} \qquad (5)$$

or the proportion of the world's income represented by country i. The v_i is a constant whose value is assumed to be less than zero.

The reason for including the p_i term is that a country's level of exports as a share of total income should change with a country's relative size. The larger the country as a proportion of the world's income, the smaller exports as a proportion of Y. Small countries will tend to be less diversified in production and therefore will rely proportionally more heavily on trade to satisfy their diverse needs. At the other extreme, a country which represents the entire world will have no exports at all, and the ratio of exports to income will be zero.

The example of the extremely large country provides the intercept value of v_i. If the country represents the entire world, $p_i = 1$, and solving for v_i in (4) yields

$$v_i = -b_i - x_i \cdot Y_i . \qquad (6)$$

Substituting this value back into (4) yields

$$\begin{aligned} X_i &= b_i + x_i \cdot Y_i - b_i \cdot p_i - x_i \cdot Y_i \cdot p_i \qquad (7) \\ &= (1-p_i) \cdot b_i + (1-p_i) \cdot x_i \cdot Y_i \end{aligned}$$

which is the final form of the export function.

The real rate of interest is incorporated through the expenditure function

$$E_i = c_i \cdot Y_i + e_i \cdot \Delta Y_i + h_i \cdot r \qquad (8)$$

where r is the real rate of interest and h_i is assumed constant and negative. Equation (8) describes the level of expenditure for a given country i. But for the world as a whole, the level of expenditure is constrained by

$$\Sigma E_i - \Sigma Y_i = 0, \ i=1, \ldots , n . \qquad (9)$$

Substituting (8) into (9) yields a world budget constraint in terms of income, changes in income and the real interest rate

$$\Sigma c_i \cdot Y_i + \Sigma e_i \cdot \Delta Y_i + \Sigma h_i \cdot r - \Sigma Y_i = 0 \ . \tag{10}$$

To simplify, all countries are assumed to have symetrical reactions, i.e. the same values of the constants. This assumption allows the equation to be solved for r,

$$r = z - cZ - e\bar{g}_w Z \tag{11}$$

where $Z = Y_i/h_i = Y_j/h_j$ and $\bar{g}_w = \Sigma \Delta Y_i / \Sigma Y_i$ or the average growth rate of income in the world. Substituting (11) into (8) yields the country expenditure function

$$E_i = c \cdot Y_i + e \cdot \Delta Y_i + h_i \cdot Z - h_i \cdot cZ - h_i \cdot e \cdot \bar{g}_w \cdot Z \ . \tag{12}$$

But since $Y_i/h_i = z$, the expression can be simplified to

$$E_i = Y_i + e \cdot (\Delta Y_i - Y_i \ \bar{g}_w) \ . \tag{13}$$

Notice that if expenditure is expressed as a ratio of income, the permanent income term ΔY_i is changed into a growth rate.

The final import function can be derived by substituting the final export equation (7) and expenditure equation (13) into the absorption relationship (3). Imports are now described by

$$M_i = (1-p_i) \cdot b_i + (1-p_i) \cdot x_i \cdot Y_i + e \cdot (\Delta Y_i - Y_i \cdot \bar{g}_w) \ . \tag{14}$$

Notice again that by expressing this equation as a fraction of income, the permanent income term changes into a growth rate.

The trade balance relation can now be derived. Subtracting imports from exports yields

$$TB_i = (1-p_i) \cdot b_i + (1-p_i) \cdot x_i \cdot Y_i - (1-p_i) \cdot b_i - (1-p_i) \cdot x_i \cdot Y_i - e \ (\Delta Y_i - Y_i \ \bar{g}_w) \ . \tag{15}$$

Notice that the Keynesian parts of the two equations (constant and Y_i terms) cancel. The resulting expression for the trade balance is

$$TB_i = -e\Delta Y_i + e \cdot Y_i \cdot \bar{g}_w \tag{16}$$

or alternatively

$$\frac{TB_i}{Y_i} = e(g_i - \bar{g}_w) \; . \tag{17}$$

Equation (17) is precisely the functional form first applied in Chapter IV.

A derivation of the same functional form in an absorption model with a Keynesian unemployment assumption is contained in Miles (1974a). The model divides goods into two groups, tradables and nontradables, and shows that a positive expenditure shock in country i will cause a relative increase in country i's growth rate and a deterioration in its trade balance. Income for country i is the value of total production

$$Y_i = P_{N/T} \cdot Y_{iN} + Y_{iT} \tag{18}$$

where $P_{N/T}$ is the price of nontradables in terms of tradables, and Y_{iN} and Y_{iT} are the production of nontradables and tradables respectively. Total expenditure is similarly defined as

$$X_i = P_{N/T} \cdot X_{iN} + X_{iT} \; . \tag{19}$$

Nontraded goods are assumed to be goods whose transportation costs are so high that they are never traded. Thus any nontraded good produced in country i must be consumed in country i. Equilibrium within the nontraded goods market therefore requires

$$P_{N/T} \cdot Y_{N/T} = P_{N/T} \cdot X_{N/T} \; . \tag{20}$$

Tradables, however, can be produced in any country. In fact the trade balance in country i will just equal the difference between production of and expenditure on tradables

$$TB_i = Y_{iT} - X_{iT} \; . \tag{21}$$

Equation (21) is simply a restatement of the basic absorption model equation. From equation (9) above it is also known that equation (21) summed across all N countries of the world must equal zero.

To simplify solving the model, two assumptions are made. First it is assumed that there exists some unemployment in all factor categories at the prevailing factor rewards. This restriction is similar to the Keynesian unemployment assumption. Because identical factors are willing to work at prevailing factor rewards, production of either good can therefore be increased at constant costs. The assumption means the relative price term $P_{N/T}$ is then assumed equal to one, and the relative price term disappears from equations (18)-(20) above.

The unemployed resources assumption also means that the real interest rate r (the marginal product of a unit of capital divided by its price) is constant. The interest rate is equivalent to the factor reward to capital. This factor reward, like all other factor rewards, is assumed to be exogenously determined and unchanging.

The second simplifying assumption is that the marginal propensity to expend out of income is zero, i.e.

$$\partial X_i / \partial Y_i = 0 \ . \qquad (22)$$

While the assumption is somewhat extreme, it does not change the final results. A zero marginal propensity to expend out of income simply precludes interaction among national incomes. If the value were not zero, a fall in country i's demand for tradables would affect country j's income, which would affect country j's demand for tradables, which would affect country i's income, etc. Such interaction among countries would greatly complicate the algebra of the model without providing any qualitative differences.

Given the assumptions of the model, the effect of a positive expenditure shock in only country i is determined.

Total expenditure in country i is equal to the expenditure function plus the component due to the exogenous shock S_i,

$$X_i = (1+S_i)\ \bar{X}_i \tag{23}$$

The change in expenditure in country i due to the shock is therefore

$$\Delta X_i = S_i \cdot \bar{X}_i > 0\ . \tag{24}$$

While in all other countries

$$\Delta X_j = S_j \cdot \bar{X}_j = 0. \tag{25}$$

The term S_i is expressed as a percentage change, so that $S_i \cdot \bar{X}_i$ is a discrete change.

The change in expenditure in country i is divided between tradables and nontradables in the fixed proportion k_i. The relationship between overall expenditure and expenditure on nontradables is

$$X_{iN} = k_i \cdot X_i \quad 0<k_i<1\ . \tag{26}$$

One would expect k_i to be a function of the relative price $P_{N/T}$. As $P_{N/T}$ rises, k_i decreases. However, since $P_{N/T}$ has been assumed constant in the model, k_i will also be a constant. Therefore when overall expenditure increases, expenditure on nontradables increases by

$$\Delta X_i^N = k_i \cdot \Delta X_i\ , \tag{27}$$

and on tradables by

$$\Delta X_i^T = (1-k_i) \cdot \Delta X_i\ . \tag{28}$$

From (20) above it is known that the demand and supply on non-tradables within a country must remain equal, so

$$\Delta X_i^N = \Delta Y_i^N\ . \tag{29}$$

Also, since the shock has occurred only in country i, production and demand for nontradables has risen only in country i, i.e.

$$\Delta X_i^N = \Delta Y_i^N > 0 = \Delta X_j^N = \Delta Y_j^N \ . \tag{30}$$

The percentage change in income from non-tradables is therefore greater in country i than in all other countries

$$\frac{\Delta Y_i^N}{Y_i^N} > 0 = \frac{\Delta Y_j^N}{Y_j^N} \tag{31}$$

On the tradables side, the total increase in world demand is equal to the increase in demand abroad and in country i,

$$\Delta X^T = \Sigma \Delta X_j^T + \Delta X_i^T \tag{32}$$

But since the shock occurs only in country i,

$$\Delta X_j^T = 0, j \neq i \tag{33}$$

and (32) reduces to

$$\Delta X^T = \Delta X_i^T \ . \tag{32'}$$

The increased demand for tradables can be supplied by any country since all countries produce tradables. All assumed distributions of the increased production would be equally arbitrary. For ease of exposition it is assumed that the increased demand is satisfied by an equiproportional increase in production in all countries. In other words,

$$\frac{\Delta Y_i^T}{Y_i^T} = \frac{\Delta Y_j^T}{Y_j^T} > 0 \ . \tag{34}$$

The equiproportional increase assumption follows directly from the fact that demand is equally likely to increase in any country.

The effect of the positive expenditure shock on growth rates can now be easily determined. The growth rate in any country equals the weighted average of the percentage change in income due to tradables and nontradables. The weights equal the percentage of total income due to each good. In country i

$$g_i = W_i^T \cdot \frac{\Delta Y_i^T}{Y_i^T} + W_i^N \cdot \frac{\Delta Y_i^N}{Y_i^N} \tag{35}$$

where $W^T = Y_i^T/Y_i$ and $W_i^N = Y_i^N/Y_i$. In all other countries,

$$g_j = W_j^T \cdot \frac{\Delta Y_j^T}{Y_j^T} + W_j^N \cdot \frac{\Delta Y_j^N}{Y_j^N} \tag{36}$$

where $W_j^T = Y_j^T/Y_j$ and $W_j^N = Y_j^N/Y_j$.

From (33) and (27) above it is known that demand and supply of nontradables increase only in country i. Therefore, comparing the rates of growth among countries,

$$g_i > g_j \; . \tag{37}$$

The rate of growth is greater in the country where the exogenous shock occurs than in any other country.[1]

The remaining problem is to determine the effect that an increase in relative growth rates will have on the trade balance. Equation (29) shows that the increased supply of nontradables will just match the increased demand. But equations (32') and (34) together show that the increased domestic supply of tradables is not sufficient to satisfy the extra demand. While the total world increase in demand for tradables occurs at home, only a fraction of the increased world supply does. The remaining demand must be satisfied from increased foreign production. In other words

$$Y_i^T - \Delta X_i^T = \Delta TB_i < 0 \rightarrow TB_j > 0 . \tag{38}$$

So a positive exogenous shock that increases domestic demand will cause the domestic country's growth rate to increase relative to that of all other countries. The

[1] There can exist a set of weights $W_j^N < W_i^N$ such that if g^T is much larger than g_i^N, then $g_i < g_j$.

exogenous shock also causes the country's trade balance to worsen. The increased relative rate of growth is associated with a trade balance worsening. A symmetric response is expected for a negative expenditure shock. Thus a negative relationship is expected between changes in growth rate differentials and changes in the trade balance.

The primary simplifying assumptions of the above model are the zero marginal propensity to expend out of income and the existence of unemployed resources. Laffer (1975c) eliminates these assumptions and presents a model of the more general case. Specifically Laffer assumes full employment in all factor categories. The full employment assumption means $P_{N/T}$ is no longer exogenous or constant. Relative price changes now are endogenous to assure proper reallocation of resources to satisfy changing demands. Relative price changes in turn can affect factor rewards, and Laffer assumes variable supplies of factors that react to the changing rewards. Finally, the marginal propensity to spend is now assumed to be greater than zero but less than one. This last assumption introduces interaction among demands and incomes of the various countries.

Laffer derives his results in terms of the same basic Keynesian model used above. Demand for both tradables and nontradables depend in the usually way on total income in the country, the rate of return to saving, government expenditure policy and the relative price of nontradables. Traded and nontraded goods are assumed imperfect substitutes in both demand and supply. The supply assumption is equivalent to assuming a unique factor of production in each industry. Possible distribution effects on demand of shifting production between traded and nontradable goods are assumed away. While the marginal propensity to spend out of income for any good is assumed less than one, the sum of the marginal propensities to spend for all goods for any one economic unit (e.g., the public, government) is assumed equal to unity.

The variable factor supply assumption is very important to Laffer's model. It is assumed that the greater factor rewards, the more factors that are willing to work and the higher is a country's income. Factor rewards can be measured in four possible ways. The factor can measure his returns in the number of traded or nontraded goods received in the present period. Alternatively the factor can measure the value of his time in terms of leisure foregone. Finally the value can be expressed as the amount of future tradables or nontradables received. With interest rate r a factor is assumed to receive 1+r units of goods for each unit of good produced this period.

The model assumes that future periods' relative prices of nontraded goods are independent of the current period's relative price. Thus given the real interest rate r, a rise in $P_{N/T}$ in the current period has no effect on the number of either future tradables or nontradables that a factor in the traded goods industry receives. But the relative price rise increases the number of future tradable and nontradable goods a factor in the nontradable goods industry can obtain. This conclusion, combined with the assumption that a rise in $P_{N/T}$ causes a shift in production towards the nontraded goods industry and that there are symmetric responses in all industries and countries to relative price changes, leads to an important result. For a given value of r, a rise in $P_{N/T}$ will cause a larger increase in the supply of nontraded goods than a fall in the supply of traded goods.

The reason for the result is that the increase in the supply of factors to the nontraded goods industry is greater than the decrease in the supply of factors to the traded goods industry. Rewards to factors in the nontraded goods industry have clearly risen. The rise in $P_{N/T}$ causes these factors to receive more present tradables and future tradables for each unit of nontradables now produced. In the traded goods industry, while factors now receive fewer nontraded goods for each unit of traded goods produced they still receive the same amount of future traded and non-traded goods. Thus factor rewards have risen more in the nontraded goods sector than they have fallen in the traded goods sector. With similar responses in both sectors, the nontraded sector expands more than the other contracts. The rise in $P_{N/T}$ therefore produces a net increase in production.

Utilizing these results, the effects of an expenditure shock are found. First the effect on growth rate differentials are found. When there is a shift in demand, the aggregate system must adjust to reinstate equilibrium in the overall goods market and the market for nontraded goods. A price change is in order. A rise in the interest rate r and relative price of nontraded goods $P_{N/T}$ will have the desired effect. The rise in r will help to reduce the excess demand in the nontraded goods sector. When expenditure rises, a portion k falls on nontraded goods and 1-k on traded goods. If it is assumed that expenditure has risen in only one country, that country will have a relative increase in the demand for its nontraded goods. The relative price $P_{N/T}$ must rise by more or fall by less in that country.

The change in both prices will have an effect on income. But since r is the same in all countries and symmetric responses are assumed to exist everywhere, the only source of differential growth rate changes is differential changes in the $P_{N/T}$'s.

An increase in $P_{N/T}$ raises Y_i in two ways. First, the increase in the price of nontradable goods raises the tradable equivalent value of the same physical output of nontradables. Second, as shown above, it causes a shift in production from tradables to nontradables and causes an increase in the total value of the factors supplied. Thus a rise in $P_{N/T}$ unambiguously raises income in terms of tradable goods. Countries with greater increases in the relative price will experience greater increases in income. The country where the expenditure shock occurs will therefore again find its growth rate increasing relative to other countries' growth rates.

Next the effect of the expenditure shock on the trade balance is determined. The country with the largest increase in $P_{N/T}$ will experience a relative worsening of the trade balance. The output of tradables will fall by more and demand for tradables rise by more in this country.

The country with the largest expenditure shock will, other things equal, also experience a relative worsening of the trade balance. The larger demand effect will result in a greater increase in demand for tradables. Furthermore, this country will have the largest increase in income, which further increases the relative demand for tradables.

Taking these results together, it is clear that the country experiencing a demand shock will have a relative worsening in its trade balance. So even within a more general Keynesian absorption model, the results are clear. Increases in the growth rate of a country relative to the rest of the world should be associated with a worsening in the ratio of the trade balance to income.

Appendix B

STATISTICAL PROPERTIES OF THE TIME SERIES DATA BY COUNTRY

The statistical properties of the various time series data used in the estimation of the equations are presented below for the fourteen countries that appear in every test. In addition to the mean and variance, estimates of significant first, second and third order autoregressive coefficients are presented. Significant autoregressive coefficients are greater than twice the estimated standard error. Insignificant coefficients are simply indicated by an asterisk (*). The symbols in the following table are:

- ARt - the estimate of the autoregressive coefficient of order t.
- TB - the change in the ratio of the trade balance to GNP.
- BOP - the change in the ratio of the balance of payments to GNP.
- G - the change in the country's growth rate differential.
- M - the change in the country's ratio of money to GNP relative to the Rest-of-World's ratio.
- GC - the change in the country's ratio of government consumption to GNP relative to the Rest-of-World's ratio.
- ER - the change in the ratio of the country's exchange rate relative to the Rest-of-World's.

Country	Variable	Mean	Variance	AR1	AR2	AR3
United Kingdom	TB	0.593 E-3	0.943 E-3			
	BOP	-0.874 E-3	0.207 E-3	-0.57	*	*
	G	-0.185 E-2	0.627 E-3	-0.46	*	*
	M	0.376 E-2	0.166 E-2	*	*	*
	GC	0.129 E-3	0.341 E-4	*	*	*
	ER	-0.308 E-4	0.136 E-7	*	*	*
Denmark	TB	0.113 E-2	0.288 E-3	*	*	*
	BOP	0.593 E-3	0.163 E-3	*	*	*
	G	-0.336 E-3	0.111 E-2	-0.48	*	*
	M	-0.335 E-3	0.137 E-3	*	*	*
	GC	0.459 E-2	0.948 E-4	*	*	*
	ER	-0.109 E-2	0.128 E-5	*	*	*
France	TB	-0.112 E-3	0.759 E-4	*	*	*
	BOP	-0.745 E-4	0.154 E-3	*	*	*
	G	-0.180 E-2	0.120 E-2	*	*	*
	M	-0.289 E-3	0.147 E-3	*	*	*
	GC	-0.974 E-3	0.416 E-4	*	*	*
	ER	0.558 E-4	0.391 E-5	*	*	*
Finland	TB	-0.133 E-2	0.251 E-3	*	-0.53	*
	BOP	-0.843 E-3	0.205 E-3	*	-0.50	*
	G	-0.230 E-2	0.130 E-2	*	-0.46	*
	M	0.103 E-2	0.119 E-3	*	*	*
	GC	0.275 E-2	0.511 E-4	*	*	*
	ER	0.329 E-3	0.446 E-5	*	*	*
Iceland	TB	0.104 E-2	0.177 E-2	*	-0.66	*
	BOP	0.314 E-3	0.682 E-3	*	-0.47	*
	G	0.122 E-2	0.528 E-2	*	*	*
	M	0.103 E-2	0.105 E-2	-0.50	-0.56	*
	GC	0.715 E-3	0.454 E-4	*	*	*
	ER	0.273 E-1	0.379 E-2	*	*	*
Ireland	TB	0.195 E-2	0.702 E-3	*	-0.57	*
	BOP	0.123 E-3	0.110 E-2	-0.58	*	*
	G	0.422 E-2	0.801 E-3	*	-0.60	*
	M	0.112 E-2	0.256 E-2	-0.55	*	*
	GC	0.164 E-2	0.671 E-4	*	*	*
	ER	-0.307 E-4	0.137 E-7	*	*	*
Spain	TB	-0.251 E-2	0.265 E-3	*	*	*
	BOP	0.166 E-2	0.149 E-3	*	*	*
	G	0.336 E-2	0.282 E-2	*	*	*
	M	0.235 E-2	0.818 E-4	*	*	*
	GC	-0.378 E-2	0.357 E-3	*	*	*
	ER	0.233 E-1	0.770 E-2	*	*	*
New Zealand	TB	0.186 E-2	0.108 E-2	*	-0.58	*
	BOP	0.229 E-2	0.316 E-3	-0.64	*	*
	G	-0.363 E-2	0.259 E-2	*	*	*
	M	-0.392 E-2	0.370 E-3	*	*	*
	GC	0.173 E-2	0.516 E-4	*	*	*
	ER	-0.698 E-4	0.577 E-7	*	*	*
Costa Rica	TB	-0.513 E-2	0.912 E-3	*	*	*
	BOP	0.677 E-3	0.346 E-3	-0.59	*	*

Country	Variable	Mean	Variance	AR1	AR2	AR3
	G	-0.380 E-2	0.136 E-2	-0.46	*	*
	M	0.267 E-2	0.119 E-3	*	*	*
	GC	0.315 E-2	0.564 E-4	*	*	*
	ER	-0.489 E-3	0.405 E-5	*	*	*
Ecuador	TB	-0.243 E-3	0.759 E-3	*	*	*
	BOP	0.208 E-2	0.251 E-3	*	*	*
	G	-0.732 E-3	0.254 E-2	*	*	*
	M	0.165 E-2	0.166 E-3	*	*	*
	GC	0.226 E-2	0.120 E-3	*	*	*
	ER	0.136 E-2	0.137 E-3	*	*	*
Guyana	TB	-0.207 E-2	0.486 E-2	*	*	*
	BOP	0.178 E-2	0.961 E-3	-0.46	*	*
	G	-0.464 E-2	0.678 E-2	*	-0.47	*
	M	0.947 E-2	0.943 E-3	*	*	*
	GC	0.469 E-2	0.164 E-3	*	*	*
	ER	-0.767 E-4	0.418 E-6	*	*	*
Israel	TB	0.153 E-2	0.123 E-2	*	*	*
	BOP	0.241 E-2	0.103 E-2	*	*	*
	G	-0.816 E-2	0.353 E-2	*	*	*
	M	0.463 E-2	0.274 E-3	*	-0.56	*
	GC	0.734 E-2	0.976 E-3	*	*	*
	ER	0.601 E-3	0.671 E-5	*	*	*
Sri Lanka	TB	-0.511 E-2	0.190 E-2	-0.46	*	*
	BOP	-0.309 E-2	0.510 E-3	*	*	*
	G	-0.681 E-2	0.301 E-2	*	*	*
	M	0.423 E-2	0.512 E-3	*	*	*
	GC	0.818 E-3	0.893 E-4	*	*	*
	ER	-0.336 E-4	0.500 E-5	*	*	*
Philippines	TB	0.119 E-3	0.381 E-3	*	-0.49	*
	BOP	0.144 E-2	0.131 E-3	-0.61	*	*
	G	0.642 E-3	0.486 E-2	*	-0.53	*
	M	0.260 E-3	0.145 E-3	*	*	*
	GC	-0.226 E-3	0.529 E-4	*	*	*
	ER	0.141 E-2	0.237 E-4	*	*	*

BIBLIOGRAPHY

Alexander, Sidney. "The Effects of Devaluation: A Simplified Synthesis of Elasticities and Absorption Approaches." *American Economic Review* 49 No. 2 (March 1959): 22-42.

_________. "The Effects of Devaluation on a Trade Balance." *International Monetary Fund Staff Papers* 2 No. 2 (April 1952): 263-78.

Andersen, Leonall C. and Jordon, Jerry L. "Monetary and Fiscal Actions: A Test of Their Relative Importance in Economic Stabilization." *Federal Reserve Bank of St. Louis Review* 50 No. 11 (November 1968): 11-23.

Black, Fischer. "The Balance of Payments in a Neoclassical Model." Mimeographed. University of Chicago, July 1973.

Connolly, Michael and Taylor, Dean. "Devaluation in Less Developed Countries." Paper prepared for conference on devaluation sponsored by the Board of Governors, Federal Reserve System, Washington, D.C., 14-15 December 1972.

Cooper, Richard, "An Assessment of Currency Devaluation in Developing Countries." In *Government and Economic Development*, Chapter 13. Edited by Gustav Ranis. Economic Growth Center, Yale University. New Haven: Yale University Press, 1971 (a).

______. "Currency Devaluation in Developing Countries." Essays in International Finance, No. 86. Princeton University Press, 1971 (a).

Dornbusch, Rudiger. "Alternative Price Stabilization Rules and the Effects of Exchange Rate Changes." Mimeograph. University of Chicago, October 1974 (a).

_________. "Currency Depreciation, Hoarding and Relative Prices." *Journal of Political Economy* 81, No. 4 (July/August 1973): 893-915 (a).

Dornbusch, Rudiger. "Devaluation, Money, and Nontraded Goods." *American Economic Review* 63 No. 5 (December 1973): 871-80 (b).

_________. "Exchange Rates and Fiscal Policy in a Popular Model of International Trade." *American Economic Review* 65 No. 5 (December 1975): 859-71 (a).

_________. "A Portfolio Balance Model of the Open Economy." *Journal of Monetary Economics* 1 (January 1975): 3-20 (b).

_________. "Real and Monetary Aspects of Exchange Rate Changes." *In National and International Monetary Policies*. Edited by Robert Z. Aliber. Chicago: University of Chicago Press, 1974 (b).

Fama, Eugene F.; Fisher, Lawrence; Jensen, Michael C.; and Roll, Richard. "The Adjustment of Stock Prices to New Information." *International Economic Review* 10 No. 1 (February 1969): 1-21.

Frenkel, Jacob and Rodriguez, Carlos. "Portfolio Equilibrium and the Balance of Payments: A Monetary Approach." *American Economic Review* 65 No. 4 (September 1975): 674-88.

Friedman, Milton. *The Optimum Quantity of Money and Other Essays*. Chicago: Aldine Publishing Company, 1969.

Haberler, Gottfried. "The Market for Foreign Exchange and the Stability of the Balance of Payments." *Kyklos* 3 No. 3 (1949): 193-218.

Johnson, Harry G. "The Monetary Approach to Balance-of-Payments Theory." *Journal of Financial and Quantitative Analysis* (March 1972): 1555-72.

_______. "Towards a General Theory of the Balance of Payments." In *International Trade and Economic Growth: Studies in Pure Theory*, Chapter VI. Cambridge: Harvard University Press, 1967.

Johnston, J. *Econometric Methods*. Second Edition. New York: McGraw-Hill, 1972.

Kmenta, Jan. *Elements of Econometrics*. New York: Macmillan, 1971.

Laffer, Arthur B. "An Anti-Traditional Theory of the Balance-of-Payments Under Fixed Exchange Rates." Mimeographed. University of Chicago, February 1969.

______. "The Economic Consequences of Devaluation of a Reserve Currency Country." Mimeographed. University of Chicago, May 1974.

______. "Exchange Rates, The Terms of Trade, and the Trade Balance." Mimeographed. University of Chicago, February 1973.

Laffer, Arthur B. "The Phenomenon of World-Wide Inflation: A Study in International Market Integration." In *The Phenomenon of World-Wide Inflation*. Edited by David Meiselman and Arthur B. Laffer. Washington, D.C.: American Enterprise Institute, 1975 (a).

______. *Private Short-Term Capital Flows*. New York: Marcel Dekker, Inc., 1975 (b).

______. "The Trade Balance and Economic Activity." Mimeographed. University of Chicago, May 1975(c).

Laffer, Arthur B. and Ranson, R. David. "Canada, the United States, and the Rest of the Developed World: A Study in the Integration of Markets." Mimeographed. University of Chicago, February 1973.

Laffer, Arthur B. and Ranson, R. David. "A Formal Model of the Economy." *The Journal of Business* 44 No. 3 (July 1971): 247-70.

Lee, Moon Hoe. *Purchasing Power Parity*. New York: Marcel Dekker, Inc., 1976.

Magee, Stephen P. "Currency Contracts, Pass-through, and Devaluation." *Brookings Papers on Economic Activity*, 1:1973, 303-23.

______. "U.S. Import Prices in the Currency-Contract Period," *Brookings Paper on Economic Activity*, 1:1974, 117-64.

Meade, J.E. *The Theory of International Economic Policy*. Vol. 1: *The Balance of Payments*. London: Oxford University Press, 1951.

Metzler, Lloyd. "The Theory of International Trade." In *A Survey of Contemporary Economics*. Edited by Howard S. Ellis. Philadelphia: Blakiston, 1948.

Miles, Marc A. "An Absorption Model of the Trade Balance." Report for U.S. Treasury Department. Mimeographed. Order No. ES 137, December 1974 (a).

______. "The Elasticities and Monetary Approaches to the Balance of Payments: A Reconciliation." Mimeographed. University of Chicago, March 1973.

______. "Re-Evaluating the Effects of Devaluation." Mimeographed. University of Chicago, October 1974 (b).

Mundell, Robert A. *International Economics*. New York: Macmillan, 1968.

______. *Monetary Theory: Inflation, Interest, and Growth in the World Economy*. Goodyear Publishing Company: Pacific Palisades, 1971.

Mussa, Michael. "Tariffs and the Balance of Payments: A Monetary Approach." In *The Monetary Approach to the Balance of Payments*. Edited by J.A. Frenkel and H.G. Johnson. London: Allen and Unwin, 1975.

Negishi, T. "Approaches to the Analysis of Devaluation." *International Economic Review* 9 No. 2 (June 1968): 218-27.

Patinkin, Don. *Money, Interest and Prices.* Second Edition. New York: Harper & Row, 1965.

Pearce, I. "The Problem of the Balance of Payments," *International Economic Review* 2 (January 1961): 1-28.

Robinson, Joan. "The Foreign Exchanges." *In Essays in the Theory of Employment.* Oxford: Blackwell, 1947.

Salant, Michael. "Devaluations Improve the Balance of Payments Even if Not the Trade Balance." Mimeographed. U.S. Treasury Department, January 1975.

Salter, W.E. "Internal and External Balance: The Role of Price and Expenditure Effects." *Economic Record* 35 (August 1959): 226-38.

Zellner, Arnold. "An Efficient Method of Estimating Seemingly Unrelated Regressions and Tests for Aggregation Bias." *Journal of the American Statistical Association* 57 (June 1962): 348-68.

INDEX